THE
HISTORY
OF
ISSUES

Crime

Other Books in the History of Issues series:

Crime

Mikko Canini, Book Editor

GREENHAVEN PRESS

An imprint of Thomson Gale, a part of The Thomson Corporation

Detroit • New York • San Francisco • New Haven, Conn. • Waterville, Maine • London

Christine Nasso, *Publisher*
Elizabeth Des Chenes, *Managing Editor*

ISBN-13: 978-0-7377-2863-7
ISBN-10: 0-7377-2863-9

Library of Congress Control Number: 2006936113

Contents

Chapter 3: Punishing Crime

Foreword

In the 1940s, at the height of the Holocaust, Jews struggled to create a nation of their own in Palestine, a region of the Middle East that at the time was controlled by Britain. The British had placed limits on Jewish immigration to Palestine, hampering efforts to provide refuge to Jews fleeing the Holocaust. In response to this and other British policies, an underground Jewish resistance group called Irgun began carrying out terrorist attacks against British targets in Palestine, including immigration, intelligence, and police offices. Most famously, the group bombed the King David Hotel in Jerusalem, the site of a British military headquarters. Although the British were warned well in advance of the attack, they failed to evacuate the building. As a result, ninety-one people were killed (including fifteen Jews) and forty-five were injured.

Early in the twentieth century, Ireland, which had long been under British rule, was split into two countries. The south, populated mostly by Catholics, eventually achieved independence and became the Republic of Ireland. Northern Ireland, mostly Protestant, remained under British control. Catholics in both the north and south opposed British control of the north, and the Irish Republican Army (IRA) sought unification of Ireland as an independent nation. In 1969, the IRA split into two factions. A new radical wing, the Provisional IRA, was created and soon undertook numerous terrorist bombings and killings throughout Northern Ireland, the Republic of Ireland, and even in England. One of its most notorious attacks was the 1974 bombing of a Birmingham, England, bar that killed nineteen people.

In the mid-1990s, an Islamic terrorist group called al Qaeda began carrying out terrorist attacks against American targets overseas. In communications to the media, the organization listed several complaints against the United States. It generally opposed all U.S. involvement and presence in the Middle East. It particularly objected to the presence of U.S. troops in Saudi Arabia, which is the home of several Islamic holy sites. And it strongly condemned the United States for supporting the nation of Israel, which it claimed was an oppressor of Muslims. In 1998 al Qaeda's leaders issued a fatwa (a religious legal statement) calling for Muslims to kill Americans. Al Qaeda acted on this order many times—most memorably on September 11, 2001, when it attacked the World Trade Center and the Pentagon, killing nearly three thousand people.

These three groups—Irgun, the Provisional IRA, and al Qaeda—have achieved varied results. Irgun's terror campaign contributed to Britain's decision to pull out of Palestine and to support the creation of Israel in 1948. The Provisional IRA's tactics kept pressure on the British, but they also alienated many would-be supporters of independence for Northern Ireland. Al Qaeda's attacks provoked a strong U.S. military response but did not lessen America's involvement in the Middle East nor weaken its support of Israel. Despite these different results, the means and goals of these groups were similar. Although they emerged in different parts of the world during different eras and in support of different causes, all three had one thing in common: They all used clandestine violence to undermine a government they deemed oppressive or illegitimate.

The destruction of oppressive governments is not the only goal of terrorism. For example, terror is also used to minimize dissent in totalitarian regimes and to promote extreme ideologies. However, throughout history the motivations of terrorists have been remarkably similar, proving the old adage that "the more things change, the more they remain the same." Arguments for and against terrorism thus boil down to the same set of universal arguments regardless of the age: Some argue that terrorism is justified to change (or, in the case of state terror, to maintain) the prevailing political order; others respond that terrorism is inhumane and unacceptable under any circumstances. These basic views transcend time and place.

Similar fundamental arguments apply to other controversial social issues. For instance, arguments over the death penalty have always featured competing views of justice. Scholars cite biblical texts to claim that a person who takes a life must forfeit his or her life, while others cite religious doctrine to support their view that only God can take a human life. These arguments have remained essentially the same throughout the centuries. Likewise, the debate over euthanasia has persisted throughout the history of Western civilization. Supporters argue that it is compassionate to end the suffering of the dying by hastening their impending death; opponents insist that it is society's duty to make the dying as comfortable as possible as death takes its natural course.

Greenhaven Press's The History of Issues series illustrates this constancy of arguments surrounding major social issues. Each volume in the series focuses on one issue—including terrorism, the death penalty, and euthanasia—and examines how the debates have both evolved and remained essentially the same over the years. Primary documents such as newspaper articles, speeches, and government reports illuminate historical developments and offer perspectives from throughout history. Secondary sources provide overviews and commentaries from a more contemporary perspective. An introduction begins each anthology and supplies essential context and background. An annotated table of contents, chronology, and index allow for easy reference, and a bibliography and list of organizations to contact point to additional sources of information on the book's topic. With these features, The History of Issues series permits readers to glimpse both the historical and contemporary dimensions of humanity's most pressing and controversial social issues.

Introduction

About thirty-five hundred years ago, Hammurabi, the ruler of the Babylonian Empire, commissioned the carving of a large stone. In so doing, he forever transformed the history of crime. The stone was inscribed with a set of laws and was placed in a public space for all to see. This was significant in that it established the principle that criminal behavior and its punishment had to be codified. Although very few of Hammurabi's subjects could read, the code ensured that the punishment of crime was spelled out and not applied arbitrarily.

Today many of the laws set forth by Hammurabi appear strange and archaic; "unjustified" curses and spells, for example, were strictly against the law. Others appear more modern, such as those concerning divorce or medical malpractice. Although the punishments proscribed by the code may seem cruel to modern readers, and sometimes wholly unjust (slaves are not governed by the same laws as their owners, for example), they reflect the society in which they were created. Ultimately, the importance of Hammurabi's code lies not in its specific dictates but rather in the fact that it reveals an ancient society's need to redress criminal acts with set punishments to deter crime and to establish a degree of formal justice.

Natural Law Versus Legal Positivism

Despite the considerable time that separates the modern legal code from that of Hammurabi, one of the fundamental problems in the understanding of crime is already apparent in this ancient text. That is, what is the basis on which people define an act as illegal? Some Babylonian laws appear "natural," such as those prohibiting physical assault, but others appear wholly contingent on the particularities of Babylonian society, such as the law that condemns to death by burning a priestess who enters a wine shop for a drink. Historically, some have argued that all legal codes must be based on a notion of "natural law," which posits an essential and immutable connection between law and justice. Yet others have argued that because humans create laws, there is no such thing as an inherently just law. This latter group forms a school of thought known as legal positivism.

The theory of natural law has a long history, but it was summed up by the thirteenth-century Catholic philosopher Saint Thomas Aquinas, who wrote that "the first precept of the law, [is] that good is to be done and promoted, and evil is to be avoided. All other precepts of the natural law are based on this." Proponents of natural law argue that there are a number of precepts that are fundamental and eternal, and that human-created laws can only be considered just insofar as they conform to these precepts. One can readily perceive the doctrine of natural law in the U.S. Declaration of Independence, which reads, "We hold these truths to be self-evident, that all men are created equal, that they are endowed by their Creator with certain unalienable Rights, that among these are Life, Liberty and the pursuit of Happiness. That to secure these rights, Governments are instituted among Men."

The concept of natural law first came under attack with the publication of English philosopher Jeremy Bentham's essay *Anarchical Fallacies*, published in 1816, in which he writes that "natural rights is simple nonsense: natural and imprescriptible rights, rhetorical nonsense, nonsense upon stilts."[1] Bentham argues that the existence of all laws can be attributed to either tradition or government, and that to think of them as deriving from either God or essential human relations prevents people from developing a coherent and sensible legal system. In opposition to the claims of the Declaration of Independence, Bentham argues that laws do not exist prior to the human institution of government, but that it is the role of government to create laws that ensure that a system of reward and punishment brings about the "greatest happiness to the greatest number of people."

Bentham's ideas, which formed the basis for legal positivism, proved highly controversial. Critics worried that without the principle of natural rights, it would be impossible to maintain a constitution, a legal code, or a civilized state. Followers of legal positivism, however, pointed to a 1762 work by the Swiss-born philosopher Jean-Jacques Rousseau. In *The Social Contract*, Rousseau claims that an ideal society is held together by a contract that binds citizens to a "general will"; it is this general will that should form the basis of the legal system, and the government's duty simply should be to enforce the laws that are proscribed by society.

Defining Crime

It would be fair to say that the American legal system comprises elements of both natural law, codified in the Bill of Rights, and legal positivism, applied under the model of a Rousseau-styled social contract. Negotiating the inherent conflicts between these two positions has proven to be an enduringly difficult task for the creators of public policy, who strive to find a balance between public demands for justice, the limits imposed by the Constitution, and the net social good of new legislation. Further complicating the struggle against crime are the diverse and competing cultural, political, and economic goals that make up American society.

In the face of these conflicting ideas about what American society is or should be, the main task of legislators becomes one of definition: to decide what is and is not a punishable crime. Of course, there is broad agreement that certain activities constitute a criminal act. Homicide—the intentional killing of a human being—is undoubtedly a crime, an understanding that both proponents of natural law and legal positivism share. The criminality of many other activities is far less certain.

For example, the criminalization of prostitution, drug use, and abortion have long incited controversy. Those who argue that such activities are inherently immoral and should be banned are applying the principle of natural law. Others argue that these activities are "victimless" insofar as they only harm the individual who chooses to engage in them. Using the principle of legal positivism, these theorists argue that these activities should not be criminalized since they do not affect the well-being of society. However, the principles of natural law and legal positivism are also deployed to argue the opposing views on these issues. Some advocates of natural law perceive the state's interference in prostitution, drug use, or abortion, for example, as contravening the more fundamental natural rights of personal liberty. Likewise, some advocates of legal positivism argue that although there may be nothing inherently wrong with these criminalized acts, in practice they result in a variety of social ills and should therefore be banned.

Determining Punishment

The position one takes in defining crime is closely tied to one's understanding of how crime should be punished. Advocates of natural law argue that punishment involves the principle of justice. Justice can be defined broadly as the morally correct assignment of good and evil. Therefore, advocates of natural law consider the deterrent effect of punishment to be secondary to the moral imperative to redress legal infractions. The best-known formulation of this concept is the Old Testament proverb "an eye for an eye, a tooth for a tooth," although this principle can be traced back to Hammurabi's code of laws. This idea is generally referred to as retributive justice, and its basic tenet is that the punishment of wrongdoing should be proportional to the severity of the crime committed. Undoubtedly, the most controversial application of this principle in America's current legal code is the application of the death penalty. Many advocates of natural law argue that a person convicted of taking the life of another should be deprived of life and that any alternative punishment will, by definition, fall short of the principle of justice.

On the other hand, advocates of legal positivism argue that the abstract ideal of justice is a human creation and that the main justification for punishment is to deter crime and perpetuate the rule of law. For them, punishment should only be as harsh as is necessary to prevent further crime. As the English philosopher Thomas Hobbes argued in 1651, "Seeing [that] the end of punishing is not revenge and discharge of choler [anger]; but correction either of the offender or of others by his example; the severest punishments are to be inflicted for those crimes that are of most danger to the public."[2] For most legal positivists, America's continued use of the death penalty reflects the desire to avenge wrongdoing and not the desire to create a safer society. As an alternative, they argue that life sentences reflect a proportional punishment and are as effective as the death penalty at protecting society. However, the increased use of life imprisonment in the American legal system has had the unintended effect of expanding America's incarceration rate, which has also become a controversial topic of discussion.

America's Growing Prison Population

America currently has the largest documented prison population in the world with 724 out of every 100,000 citizens living in correctional facilities. The rapidly growing prison population, which has mushroomed since 1971 when the rate was only 96 per 100,000 citizens, has become a highly controversial issue, with all sides of the debate using arguments based on both natural law and legal positivism.

Some proponents of natural-law theory argue that America's high incidence of incarceration must mean that the current legal system no longer reflects natural law. They point to statistics that demonstrate that a black male has about a one in three chance of going to prison in his lifetime, a Hispanic male one in six, and a white male one in seventeen, as evidence that the principle of justice is no longer being upheld. Others argue that the increasing prison rate simply reflects a growing lawlessness in society brought about by the breakdown of social bonds, the celebration of criminality in the media, or even the existence of the welfare state.

From the perspective of legal positivism, the principle argument for maintaining a high rate of incarceration links the increase in imprisonment with the decline in the crime rate. Contrary to popular perception, the crime rate in the United States fell consistently every year from 1992, with violent crime reaching the lowest level ever recorded in 2004 (though more recently, the rates have experienced an upward movement). For many, this decrease in the crime rate was directly attributable to the increasing incarceration rate. As Assistant Attorney General Christopher A. Wray stated in 2005, "Tough sentencing means less crime.... [Tough federal sentencing guidelines] have helped reduce crime by ensuring that criminal sentences take violent offenders off the streets, impose just punishment and deter others from committing crimes."[3]

Although Wray's statement speaks to the commonsense idea that the threat of punishment deters crime, many have questioned whether punishment does in fact have a deterrent effect. The most widely cited study on this question was conducted by economics professor Isaac Ehrlich in 1973. Ehrlich's "Participation in Illegitimate Activities: An Economic Analysis" found that crime rates were directly tied to both the likelihood of serving time in prison and the average length of the sentence. However, in the two decades following Ehrlich's study, the prison population more than tripled while violent crimes doubled on a per capita basis, leading many to argue that the threat of imprisonment does not have a significant deterrent effect. As criminologists James Austin and Marc

Mauer argued in a 1994 *USA Today* article, "The states with the lowest crime rates have the lowest imprisonment rates, and states with the highest crime rates have the highest imprisonment rates. There is no evidence that imprisonment reduces crime."[4]

Even if one could determine that a quantifiable causal relationship exists between punishment and deterrence, many have rightly pointed out that this would not effectively address the problem of determining just sentences. They argue that America's booming incarceration rate is partly the effect of unduly long sentences meted out to criminals by a legal system desperate to appear tough on crime. They point to a 1993 study commissioned by the National Research Council that found that "a 50 percent increase in the *probability of incarceration* would prevent twice as much violent crime as a 50 percent increase in the average term of incarceration."[5]

The Police Presence

The idea that criminals are more deterred by the likelihood of punishment than by the severity of the punishment finds its roots in a 1968 paper by the economist Gary S. Becker. Titled "Crime and Punishment: An Economic Approach," it argues that criminal behavior results from rational calculations that compare the possible benefits of a criminal act with the probability and cost of being apprehended and punished. Becker's thesis proved highly controversial. At the time, most criminologists believed that criminal behavior was the result of mental illness or social oppression, but for Becker, "some persons become 'criminals' . . . not because their basic motivation differs from that of other persons, but because their benefits and costs differ."[6]

Following Becker's conclusion, many have argued that the most effective way to reduce crime is to increase the rate of apprehension and that this can only be achieved by hiring more police officers. However, those who argue that more police presence means less crime have long had difficulty finding evidence to prove their thesis. Statistical analysis has consistently failed to find a causal link between increased police presence and decreased crime rates. In fact, many studies find that increases in the size of police forces seem to match increases in crime, though these findings are generally assumed to result from the fact that increasing crime rates are often accompanied by police hiring or because an increase in police officers leads to an increase in the reporting of crime.

Those who favor an increased police presence despite this lack of statistical evidence offer a simple proposition to back their claims: If every single crime committed resulted in the apprehension of the perpetrator and the imposition of a stiff sentence, crime would virtually disappear overnight. Therefore, the more police the country has, the more arrests will be made and the less crime society will have to endure. Although this proposition is hypothetical, it does raise a fundamental question concerning crime—that is, how much crime are Americans willing to accept? While hiring more and more police officers and developing harsher and longer sentences may well bring about a reduction in crime, the consequences of such actions would result in a society devoid of the liberties that proponents of both natural law and legal positivism seek to safeguard. As Benjamin Franklin wrote in 1755, "Those who would give up essential liberty to purchase a little temporary safety, deserve neither liberty nor safety."[7] America continues to struggle with this fundamental dilemma as well as all the other controversies that affect lawmakers' attempts to balance the punishing of criminal acts against the preservation of social liberties.

Notes

1. Jeremy Bentham, "Anarchical Fallacies," in *The Works of Jeremy Bentham*, ed. John Bowring. Edinburgh: William Tait, 1843, p. 501.
2. Thomas Hobbes, *Hobbe's Leviathan: Reprinted from the Edition of 1651*. Oxford, UK: Clarendon, 1909, p. 269.

3. Christopher A. Wray, "Prepared Remarks of Assistant Attorney General Christopher A. Wray, Response to *Booker/Fanfan*." Washington, DC, January 12, 2005. www.usdoj.gov/criminal/press_room/press_releases/2005_3131_WraySentencing Guidelinesfinalformatted.pdf.

4. James Austin and Marc Mauer, "'Crime Explosion' Is a Myth," *USA Today*, January 27, 1994, p. 13A.

5. Albert J. Reiss Jr. and Jeffrey A. Roth, eds., *Understanding and Preventing Violence.* Washington, DC: National Academy, 1993, p. 6.

6. Gary S. Becker, "Crime and Punishment: An Economic Approach," *Journal of Political Economy*, March/April 1968, pp. 169–217.

7. Benjamin Franklin, "Pennsylvania Assembly: Reply to the Governor, November 11, 1755," in *The Papers of Benjamin Franklin*, vol. 6, ed. Leonard W. Labaree. New Haven, CT: Yale University Press, 1963, p. 242.

CHAPTER 1

The Causes of Crime

Chapter Preface

On January 20, 1692, in Salem Village, Massachusetts, two young girls began exhibiting strange behavior: contorting their bodies, screaming, crawling under furniture, and uttering strange sounds. It was decided by the local doctor, ministers, and townspeople that witchcraft was the cause of their inexplicable behavior, and when questioned, the girls accused three local women of bewitching them. This was a very serious charge; in seventeenth-century New England witchcraft was considered a capital crime. In the ensuing hysteria, some twenty people were accused, tried, and executed for practicing witchcraft, and local prisons were filled to capacity with suspected practitioners.

The source of the community's fear was the idea, prevalent until the end of the eighteenth century, that deviant, sinful, or criminal behavior was caused by demonic possession or other supernatural forces. From this viewpoint, the punishing of crime was literally an embodiment of the community's struggle against the forces of evil. However, the Enlightenment supplanted such beliefs in the cause of criminal behavior with the idea that God endowed humans with rational free will. Rationalist philosophers such as Cesare Beccaria (1738–1794) and Jeremy Bentham (1748–1832) persuaded society that individuals were responsible for their own actions. Furthermore, they argued that crime was the result of a rational decision based on a calculation of costs and benefits. Quite simply, people would engage in criminal acts if the potential gain outweighed the risk of punishment.

If the rationalist thinkers were correct about the root cause of crime—that is, rational calculation—the reduction of crime would be a simple matter of making the legal system more punitive. However, such changes in the legal system did not have a significant impact on the increasing crime rate, and by the end of the nineteenth century a new perspective on deviant behavior took hold. Known as the biological or pathological school, prominent thinkers who championed this perspective argued that crime was the result of abnormal brain functioning. This represented a radical break with rationalist thought in two ways. First, criminals were supposedly "born to be bad" and could not be deterred by a well-considered legal system. Second, scientists could detect "criminal types" through careful analysis and measurement, ultimately identifying a criminal before a crime had even been committed. The approach of the pathological school had many disturbing consequences. Following the recently published theory of evolution (Charles Darwin's 1859 *Origin of Species*), some criminologists argued that the obvious solution to the crime problem was forced sterilization, eugenics, and genocide.

The inherent limitations and ethical consequences of the pathological school soon gave way to a new body of thought that emphasized the ways that individuals are socialized, particularly during childhood. The fundamental principle of the social interaction school of crime theory is that criminals are created by society. Thus, although most individuals are socialized effectively to follow social conventions, a minority lack this social conditioning and engage in criminal behavior. Although the theories to explain why some are less conditioned than others to obey the law are myriad, what they share is the idea that the root cause of criminal behavior is social, and it is only fundamental changes in society that will reduce crime. It is this body of sociological thought that most informs twentieth-century criminology. However, some of the concepts associated with the rationalist and pathological theories still can be found in contemporary accounts of the causes of crime.

Poverty Creates Crime

Clarence Darrow

It has become commonplace to remark that there is a correlation between poverty and crime. Numerous studies have revealed that demographic and social conditions have a determining effect on criminality; that is, children who live in poverty are more likely to engage in criminal activity later in life. However, conservative critics argue that this relationship is not causal; people do not commit crime because they are poor, but criminals are poor because they are predisposed to commit crime. This view, that there is a criminal "type" born without the moral fortitude to comply with society's laws, was common at the beginning of the twentieth century when the famous criminal lawyer Clarence Darrow wrote the following essay.

Darrow's principle thesis that poverty creates crime is unique in that he defines crime as a business. Darrow is concerned with countering the idea that criminal behavior is the result of moral weakness, instead arguing that crime is a trade born out of necessity for those whose position in society allows no hope for wealth or prosperity. From this analysis Darrow concludes that the only way to reduce crime is to create a better education system and a fairer society that rewards not only professional work, but the manual labor generally performed by the poor.

Those who have had no experience in the courts and no knowledge of what is known as the "criminal class" have a general idea that a criminal is not like other men. The people they know are law-abiding, conventional believers in the State and the Church and all social customs and relations; they have strict ideas of property rights, and regard the law as sacred. True, they have no more acquaintance with law-makers and politicians in general than with the criminal class, which,

Clarence Darrow, *Crime: Its Cause and Treatment*. New York: Thomas Y. Crowell, 1922.

of course, is one reason why they have such unbounded confidence in the law. Such persons are surprised and shocked when some member of the family or some friend is entangled in the courts, and generally regard it as a catastrophe that has come upon him by accident or a terrible mistake. As a rule, they do all in their power to help him whether he is acquitted or convicted. They never think that he and everyone else they know is not materially different from the ordinary criminal. As a matter of fact, the potential criminal is in every man, and no one was ever so abandoned that some friend would not plead for him, or that someone who knew him would not testify to his good deeds.

The Childhood of the Criminal

The criminal is not hard to understand. He is one who, from inherited defects or from great misfortune or especially hard circumstances, is not able to make the necessary adjustments to fit him to his environment. Seldom is he a man of average intelligence, unless he belongs to a certain class that will be discussed later. Almost always he is below the normal intelligence, and in perhaps half of the cases, very much below. Nearly always he is a person of practically no education and no property. One who has given attention to the subject of crime knows exactly where the criminal comes from and how he will develop. The crimes of violence and murder, and the lesser crimes against property, practically all come from those who have been reared in the poor and congested districts of cities and large villages. The robbers, burglars, pickpockets and thieves are from these surroundings. In a broad sense, some criminals are born and some are made. Nearly all of them are both born and made. This does not mean that criminality can be inherited, or even that there is a criminal type. It means that with certain physical and mental imperfections and with certain environment the criminal will be the result.

Seldom does one begin a criminal life as a full-grown man. The origin of the typical criminal is an imperfect child, suffering from some defect. Usually he was born with a weak intellect, or an unstable nervous system. He comes from poor parents. Often one or both of these died or met misfortune while he was young. He comes from the crossed part of a poor district. He has had little chance to go to school and could not have been a scholar, no matter how regularly he attended school. Some useful things he could have learned had society furnished the right teachers, surroundings and opportunities to make the most of an imperfect child. . . .

Naturally he has no strong sense of property rights. He has always had a hard time to get enough to eat and wear, and he has grown up unconsciously to see the inequality of distribution and to believe that it is not fair and that there is little or no justice in the world. As a child he learned to get things the best way he could, and to think nothing about it. In short, his life, like all other lives, moves along the lines of least resistance. He soon comes to feel that the police are his natural enemies and his chief business is to keep from getting caught. Inevitably he is brought into the Juvenile Court. He may be reprimanded at first. He comes again and is placed on probation. The next time he goes to a Juvenile Prison, where he can learn all the things he has not found out before. He is known to the police, known to the Court, known to the neighbors. His status is fixed. When released from prison, he takes his old heredity back into his old environment. It is the easiest to him, for he has learned to make his adjustments to this environment. From fifteen to twenty-five years of age, he has the added burden of adolescence, the trying time in a boy's life when sex feelings are developing, when he is passing from childhood to manhood. This is a very difficult time at best to the type of boy from which a criminal grows; he meets it without preparation or instruction. What he knows he learns from others like himself. He gets weird, fantastic, neurotic ideas, which only add to his natural wonderment.

The Criminal Trades

Every person who has not inherited property must live by some trade or calling. Very few people in jail or out choose their profession. Even if one selects his profession, it does not follow that he has chosen the calling for which he is best adapted. So far as a person can and does follow his desires, he generally means to choose the calling which will bring him the greatest amount of return for the least exertion. He may have strong inclinations in certain directions, as, for instance, to paint or to write or to investigate or to philosophize, but as a rule, he does not make his living from following these ambitions. If he does, it is generally a poor living. But usually his aim is to make money at something else so that he can give free rein to his real ambitions. . . .

The chances are great that he will never find what he wants; that he has not had the preparation or training for a successful workingman's career, whatever that might be. He is a doer of odd jobs and of poorly paid work all his life.

He must have some calling and takes the easiest one, which is often a life of crime. From this start comes the professional criminal, so-called. He may make a business of picking pockets. If this comes to be his trade it is very hard for him to give it up. There is so strong an element of chance—he never knows what a pocket will contain—it gratifies a spirit of adventure. Then it is easy. The wages are much greater than he could get in any other calling; the hours are short and it never interferes with his amusements. It is not so dangerous as being a burglar or a switchman, for he can find an excuse for jostling one in the street-cars or in a crowd and thus reaching into a pocket.

The burglar is not so apt to be a professional; his is a bolder and more hazardous trade; if he is caught he is taken from his occupation for a longer time. The great hazard involved in this trade and also the physical strength and fitness of those who follow it lead to its abandonment more frequently than is the case with a pickpocket or a petty thief. Robbery is seldom a profession. It is usually the crime of the young and venturesome and almost surely leads to early disaster. Murder, of course, is never a profession. In a broad way it is the result of accident or passion, or of relations which are too hard to endure.

Poverty Creates Crime

In prison and out, I have talked with scores of these men and boys. I am sure they rarely tried to deceive me. I have very seldom seen one who felt that he had done wrong, or had any thought of what the world calls reformation. A very few have used the current language of those who talk of reform, but generally they were the weakest and most hopeless of the lot and usually adopted this attitude to deceive. In almost every instance where you meet any sign of intelligence, excuses and explanations are freely made, and these explanations fully justify their points of view. Often too they tell you in sincerity that they believe their way of life is too hard and does not pay; that while they cannot see how they could have done any differently in the past, they believe their experience has taught them to stick by the rules of the game.

The boy delinquent grows naturally and almost inevitably into the man criminal. He has generally never learned a trade. No habits have been formed in his youth to keep him from crime. A life of crime is the only one open to him, and for this life he has had ample experience, inclination and opportunity. Then, too, for this kind of young man, the life of a criminal has a strong appeal. Life without opportunity and without a gambler's chance to win a considerable prize is not attractive to anyone. The conventional man who devotes his life to business or to a profession always has before him the prizes of success—to some honor and glory, and to most of them wealth. Imagine the number of lawyers, doctors and businessmen who could stick to a narrow path if they knew that life offered no opportunity but drudgery and poverty! Nearly all of these look forward to the prizes of success. Most of them expect success and many get it. For the man that I have described, a life of toil offers no chance of success.

The man grown from boyhood into ways of vice and crime sees this hope and this hope only to make a strike. He has no strong convictions and no well-settled habits to hold him back. The fear of the law only means greater caution, and after all he has nothing to lose. In his world, arrest and conviction do not mean loss of caste; they mean only bad luck. With large numbers of men crime becomes a trade. It grows to be a business as naturally as any other calling comes to be a trade. . . .

Society Is to Blame

There are professional criminals of a different grade, like the forger and the confidence man. Both of these have generally had some education and a fair degree of intelligence, and have had some advantages in life. The forger, as a rule, is a bookkeeper or an accountant who grows expert with the pen. He works for a small salary and sees nothing better. He grows familiar with signatures. Sometimes he is a clerk in a bank and has the opportunity to study signatures; he begins to imitate them, often with no thought of forging paper. He does it because it is an art and probably the only thing he can do well. Perhaps some hard luck or an unfortunate venture on the Board of Trade, or in a faro bank [at a card game], makes him write a check or note. He easily convinces himself that he is not getting the salary he earns and that less worthy men prosper while he is poor. Then too his business calls for better clothes and better surroundings than those of the working-man, and gives him many glimpses of easy lives. For a time he may escape. If the amount is not too large it is often passed by without an effort to detect. Sometimes it escapes notice altogether. Some businessmen write so many checks that they take no pains at the end of the month to figure up their account and examine every check, and never notice it unless the balance given by the bank is so far out of the way that it attracts attention. After a forger grows to be an expert, he can move from town to town. If he is taken and put in prison and finally released, he is hard to cure. Forgery is too easy and he knows of no other trade so good. A large percentage of these men never would have forged, had their wages been higher. Many others are the victims of the get-rich-quick disease; they haunt the gambling houses, brokers' offices and the like. Often when they begin they expect to make the check good; generally, they would have made good if the right card had only turned up in the faro bank, or the right quotation on the stock exchange. . . .

But with few exceptions, the criminal comes from the walks of the poor and has no education or next to none. For this, society is much to blame. Sometimes he is obliged to go to work too soon, but often he cannot learn at school. This is not entirely the fault of the boy's heredity; it is largely the fault of the school. A certain course of study has been laid out. With only slight changes, this course has come down from the past and is fixed and formal. Much of it might be of value to a professional man, but most of it is of no value to the man in other walks of life. Because a boy cannot learn arithmetic, grammar or geography, or not even learn to read and write, it does not follow that he cannot learn at all. He may possibly have marked mechanical ability; he may have more than the ordinary powers of adaptation to many kinds of work. These he could be taught to do and often to do well. Under proper instruction he might become greatly interested in some kind of work, and in the study to prepare him for the work. Then too it is more or less misleading to say that an uneducated man commits crime because he is uneducated. Often his lack of education as well as his crime comes from poverty. Crime and poverty may come from something else. All come because he had a poor make-up or an insufficient chance.

After all, the great majority of men must do some kind of manual labor. Until the time shall come when this kind of work is as easy and as well paid as other employment, no one will do manual labor if he can do any other kind. Perhaps the time may come when the hardest and most disagreeable work will be the best paid. There are too many unskilled workers in proportion to the population to make this seem very near. In the meantime—and that is doubtless a long time—someone must do this work. Much of it is done under supervision and requires no great skill and need not be very disagreeable or hard. In a complex civilization there is room for everyone to contribute to the whole. If our schools are someday what they should be, a large part of their time, in some cases all of it, will be devoted to manual training and will be given to producing skilled workmen. This sort of school work can be made attractive to thousands of boys who can do nothing else. And if easier conditions of life under fairer social surroundings could be added to this kind of education, most boys who now drift into crime would doubtless find the conventional life more profitable and attractive.

White Collar Crime Needs to Be Addressed

Edwin H. Sutherland

In December 1939, criminologist Edwin H. Sutherland delivered the following presidential address to the American Sociological Society, in which he coins the term "white-collar crime." In what was to become a historic speech, Sutherland proposes a controversial thesis: that crime is not the result of the biological and emotional conditions associated with poverty, but that it is a learned behavior that is exhibited with equal intensity in the business and professional classes. Sutherland argues that sociologists had made a false link between poverty and crime precisely because those types of criminal activities that were available to the poor happened also to be very visible and easily detectable, and because the crimes committed by the professional classes were generally not regarded as crimes.

Sutherland analyzes a variety of activities, such as fraud, embezzlement, and fee-splitting, and concludes not only that the financial cost of white-collar crime is many times that of "regular" crime, but that such activities ought to be dealt with in the criminal justice system. This was a novel idea, because, at the time, the crimes of the upper classes were generally dealt with through civil courts or administrative boards and were rarely accompanied by sanctions other than warnings, the loss of a professional license, or the occasional fine. Ultimately, Sutherland was concerned with expanding the definition of crime in order to negate the preferential treatment those of the uppor socioeconomic classes experienced in the justice system.

The criminal statistics show unequivocally that crime, *as popularly conceived and officially measured*, has a high incidence in the lower class and a low incidence in the upper

Edwin H. Sutherland, "White-Collar Criminality," *American Sociological Review*, vol. 5, no. 1, February 1940, pp. 1–12.

class; less than two percent of the persons committed to prisons in a year belong to the upper class. These statistics refer to criminals handled by the police, the criminal and juvenile courts, and the prisons, and to such crimes as murder, assault, burglary, robbery, larceny, sex offenses, and drunkenness, but exclude traffic violations.

The criminologists have used the case histories and criminal statistics derived from these agencies of criminal justice as their principal data. From them, they have derived general theories of criminal behavior. These theories are that, since crime is concentrated in the lower class, it is caused by poverty or by personal and social characteristics believed to be associated statistically with poverty, including feeblemindedness, psychopathic deviations, slum neighborhoods, and "deteriorated" families. This statement, of courses, does not do justice to the qualifications and variations in the conventional theories of criminal behavior, but it presents correctly their central tendency.

The thesis of this paper is that the conception and explanations of crime which have just been described are misleading and incorrect, that crime is in fact not closely correlated with poverty or with the psychopathic and sociopathic conditions associated with poverty, and that an adequate explanation of criminal behavior must proceed along quite different lines. The conventional explanations are invalid principally because they are derived from biased samples. The samples are biased in that they have not included vast areas of criminal behavior of persons not in the lower class. One of these neglected areas is the criminal behavior of business and professional men, which will be analyzed in this paper. . . .

The Legitimate Rackets

White-collar criminality in business is expressed most frequently in the form of misrepresentation in financial statements of corporations, manipulation in the stock exchange, commercial bribery, bribery of public officials directly or indirectly in order to secure favorable contracts and legislation, misrepresentation in advertising and salesmanship, embezzlement and misapplication of funds, short weights and measures and misgrading of commodities, tax frauds, misapplication of funds in receiverships, and bankruptcies. These are what [notorious gangster] Al Capone called "the legitimate rackets." These and many others are found in abundance in the business world.

In the medical profession, which is here used as an example because it is probably less criminalistic than some other professions, are found illegal sale of alcohol and narcotics, abortion, illegal services to underworld criminals, fraudulent reports and testimony in accident cases, extreme cases of unnecessary treatment, fake specialists, restriction of competition, and fee-splitting. Fee-splitting is a violation of a specific law in many states and a violation of the conditions of admission to the practice of medicine in all. The physician who participates in fee-splitting tends to send his patients to the surgeon who will give him the largest fee rather than to the surgeon who will do the best work. It has been reported that two-thirds of the surgeons in New York City split fees, and that more than one half of the physicians in a central western city who answered a questionnaire on this point favored fee-splitting.

These varied types of white-collar crimes in business and the professions consist principally of violation of delegated or implied trust, and many of them can be reduced to two categories: misrepresentation of asset values and duplicity in the manipulation of power. The first is approximately the same as fraud or swindling; the second is similar to the double-cross. The latter is illustrated by the corporation director who, acting on inside information, purchases land which the corporation will need and sells it at a fantastic profit to his corporation. The principle of this duplicity is that the offender holds two antagonistic positions, one of which is a position of trust, which is violated, generally by misapplication of funds, in the interest of the other position. A football coach, permitted to referee a game in which his own team was playing, would illustrate this antagonism of positions. Such situations cannot be completely avoided in a complicated business structure, but many concerns make a practice of assuming such antagonistic functions and regularly violating the trust thus delegated to them. When compelled by law to make a separation of their functions, they make a nominal separation and continue by subterfuge to maintain the two positions. . . .

The Costs of White-Collar Crime

The financial cost of white-collar crime is probably several times as great as the financial cost of all the crimes which are customarily regarded as the "crime problem." An officer of a chain grocery store in one year embezzled $600,000, which was six times as much as the annual losses from five hundred burglaries and robberies of the stores in that chain. Public enemies numbered one to six secured $130,000 by burglary and robbery in 1938. . . . *The New York Times* in 1931 reported four cases of embezzlement in the United States with a loss of more than a million dollars each and a combined loss of nine million dollars. Although a million-dollar burglar or robber is practically unheard of, these million-dollar embezzlers are small-fry among white-collar criminals. The estimated loss to investors in one investment trust from 1929 to 1935 was $580,000,000, due primarily to the fact that 75 percent of the values in the portfolio were in securities of affiliated companies, although it advertised the importance of diversification in investments and its expert services in selecting safe securities. In Chicago, the claim was made six years ago that householders had lost $54,000,000 in two years during the administration of a city sealer who granted immunity from inspection to stores which provided Christmas baskets for his constituents.

The financial loss from white-collar crime, great as it is, is less important than the damage to social relations. White-collar crimes violate trust and therefore create distrust, which lowers social morale and produces social disorganization on a large scale. Other crimes produce relatively little effect on social institutions or social organization.

White-collar crime is real crime. It is not ordinarily called crime, and calling it by this name does not make it worse, just as refraining from calling it crime does not make it better than it otherwise would be. It is called crime here in order to bring it within the scope of criminology, which is justified because it is in violation of the criminal law. The crucial question in this analysis is the criterion of violation of the criminal law. Conviction in the criminal court, which is sometimes suggested as the criterion, is not adequate because a large proportion of those who commit crimes are not convicted in criminal courts. . . .

Poverty Does Not Create Crime

The theory that criminal behavior in general is due either to poverty or to the psychopathic and sociopathic conditions associated with poverty can now be shown to be invalid for three reasons. First, the generalization is based on a biased sample which omits almost entirely the behavior of white-collar criminals. The criminologists have restricted their data, for reasons of convenience and ignorance rather than of principle, largely to cases dealt with in criminal courts and juvenile courts, and these agencies are used principally for criminals from the lower economic strata. Consequently, their data are grossly biased from the point of view of the economic status of criminals and their generalization that criminality is closely associated with poverty is not justified.

Second, the generalization that criminality is closely associated with poverty obviously does not apply to white-collar criminals. With a small number of exceptions, they are not in poverty, were not reared in slums or badly deteriorated families, and are not feebleminded or psychopathic. They were seldom problem children in their earlier years and did not appear in juvenile courts or child guidance clinics. The proposition, derived from the data used by the conventional criminologists, that "the criminal of today was the problem child of yesterday" is seldom true of white-collar criminals. The idea that the causes of criminality are to be found almost exclusively in childhood similarly is fallacious. Even if poverty is extended to include the economic stresses which afflict business in a period of depression, it is not closely correlated with white-collar criminality. Probably at no time within fifty years have white-collar crimes in the field of investments and of corporate management been so extensive as during the boom period of the twenties.

Third, the conventional theories do not even explain lower-class criminality. The sociopathic and psychopathic factors which have been emphasized doubtless have something to do with crime causation, but these factors have not been related to a general process which is found both in white-collar criminality and lower-class criminality and therefore they do not explain the criminality of either class. They may explain the manner or method of crime—why lower-class criminals commit burglary or robbery rather than false pretenses. . . .

Crime Is Learned Behavior

The hypothesis which is here suggested as a substitute for the conventional theories is that white-collar criminality, just as other systematic criminality, is learned; that it is learned in direct or indirect association with those who already practice the behavior; and that those who learn this criminal behavior are segregated from frequent and intimate contacts with law-abiding behavior. Whether a person becomes a criminal or not is determined largely by the comparative frequency and intimacy of his contacts with the two types of behavior. This may be called the process of differential association. It is a genetic explanation both of white-collar criminality and lower-class criminality. Those who become white-collar criminals generally start their careers in good neighborhoods and good homes, graduate from colleges with some idealism, and with little selection on their part, get into particular business situations in which criminality is practically a folkway, and are inducted into that system of behavior just as into any other folkway. The lower-class criminals generally start their careers in deteriorated neighborhoods and families, find delinquents at hand from whom they acquire the attitudes toward, and techniques of, crime through association with delinquents and in partial segregation from law-abiding people. The essentials of the process are the same for the two classes of criminals. This is not entirely a process of assimilation, for inventions are frequently made, perhaps more frequently in white-collar crime than in lower-class crime. The inventive geniuses for the lower-class criminals are generally professional criminals, while the inventive geniuses for many kinds of white-collar crime are generally lawyers.

A second general process is social disorganization in the community. Differential association culminates in crime because the community is not organized solidly against that behavior. The law is pressing in one direction, and other forces are pressing in the opposite direction. In business, the "rules of the game" conflict with the legal rules. A businessman who wants to obey the law is driven by his competitors to adopt their methods. This is well illustrated by the persistence of commercial bribery in spite of the strenuous efforts of business organizations to eliminate it. Groups and individuals are individuated; they are more concerned with their specialized group or individual interests than with the larger welfare. Consequently, it is not possible for the community to present a solid front in opposition to crime. The Better Business Bureaus and Crime Commissions, composed of business and professional men, attack burglary, robbery, and cheap swindles, but overlook the crimes of their own members. The forces which impinge on the lower class are similarly in conflict. Social disorganization affects the two classes in similar ways.

Unchecked Minor Crimes
Lead to Lawlessness

George L. Kelling and James Q. Wilson

In 1993, newly elected New York City mayor Rudy Giuliani implemented an aggressive policing strategy known as "zero tolerance." Under the policy, laws concerning minor offenses such as turnstile jumping, jaywalking, and public drunkenness would be strictly enforced. He argued that a crackdown on this type of minor criminal behavior would create an atmosphere of lawfulness and would result in the decrease of more serious crimes. Following the implementation of this policy, New York's crime rate did fall dramatically, though critics argued that the cause of this drop was not tougher policing but the demographic changes that had led to a drop in nationwide crime rates during the same period. Others argued that the fall was not the result of "zero tolerance," but the employment of 5,000 new police officers and the implementation of smarter policing strategies.

Giuliani's policy was based on the following theory published by public-policy professors George L. Kelling and James Q. Wilson in 1982. Named "broken windows," the theory proposes that crime is the result of the perception of lawlessness created by minor offenses like vandalism. Kelling and Wilson argue that in order to maintain a strict sense of public order, increased police foot patrols with a close familiarity with their assigned neighborhoods are required. Furthermore, these officers should return to an "old-fashioned" type of police work whereby legal and "extralegal" steps are taken to ensure that the community's standards are upheld. Critics argued that the type of policing Kelling and

George L. Kelling and James Q. Wilson, "Broken Windows: The Police and Neighborhood Safety," *Atlantic Monthly*, vol. 249, March 1982, pp. 29–38. Copyright © 1982 by the Atlantic Monthly Group. All rights reserved. Reproduced by permission of the author.

Wilson champion would lead to the curtailing of civil liberties and the harassment of minorities and those seen as socially undesirable.

In the mid-1970s, the State of New Jersey announced a "Safe and Clean Neighborhoods Program," designed to improve the quality of community life in twenty-eight cities. As part of that program, the state provided money to help cities take police officers out of their patrol cars and assign them to walking beats. The governor and other state officials were enthusiastic about using foot patrol as a way of cutting crime, but many police chiefs were skeptical. Foot patrol, in their eyes, had been pretty much discredited. It reduced the mobility of the police, who thus had difficulty responding to citizen calls for service, and it weakened headquarters control over patrol officers.

Many police officers also disliked foot patrol, but for different reasons: it was hard work, it kept them outside on cold, rainy nights, and it reduced their chances for making a "good pinch." In some departments, assigning officers to foot patrol had been used as a form of punishment. And academic experts on policing doubted that foot patrol would have any impact on crime rates; it was, in the opinion of most, little more than a sop to public opinion. But since the state was paying for it, the local authorities were willing to go along.

Public Perceptions of Safety

Five years after the program started, the Police Foundation, in Washington, D.C., published an evaluation of the foot-patrol project. Based on its analysis of a carefully controlled experiment carried out chiefly in Newark, the foundation concluded, to the surprise of hardly anyone, that foot patrol had not reduced crime rates. But residents of the foot-patrolled neighborhoods seemed to feel more secure than persons in other areas, tended to believe that crime had been reduced, and seemed to take fewer steps to protect themselves from crime (staying at home with the doors locked, for example). Moreover, citizens in the foot-patrol areas had a more favorable opinion of the police than did those living elsewhere. And officers walking beats had higher morale, greater job satisfaction, and a more favorable attitude toward citizens in their neighborhoods than did officers assigned to patrol cars.

These findings may be taken as evidence that the skeptics were right—foot patrol has no effect on crime; it merely fools the citizens into thinking that they are safer. But in our view, and in the view of the authors of the Police Foundation study (of whom [author George] Kelling was one), the citizens of Newark were not fooled at all. They knew what the foot-patrol officers were doing, they knew it was different from what motorized officers do, and they knew that having officers walk beats did in fact make their neighborhoods safer.

Neighborhood Rules

But how can a neighborhood be "safer" when the crime rate has not gone down—in fact, may have gone up? Finding the answer requires first that we understand what most often frightens people in public places. Many citizens, of course, are primarily frightened by crime, especially crime involving a sudden, violent attack by a stranger. This risk is very real, in Newark as in many large cities. But we tend to overlook another source of fear—the fear of being bothered by disorderly people. Not violent people nor, necessarily, criminals, but disreputable or obstreperous or unpredictable people: panhandlers, drunks, addicts, rowdy teenagers, prostitutes, loiterers, the mentally disturbed.

What foot-patrol officers did was to elevate, to the extent they could, the level of public order in these neighborhoods. Though the neighborhoods were predominantly black and the foot patrolmen were mostly white, this "order-maintenance" function of the police was performed to the general satisfaction of both parties. . . .

The people on the street were primarily black; the officer who walked the street was white. The people were made up of "regulars" and "strangers." Regulars included both "decent folk" and some drunks and derelicts who were always there but who "knew their place." Strangers were, well, strangers, and viewed suspiciously, sometimes apprehensively. The officer—call him Kelly—knew who the regulars were, and they knew him. As he saw his job, he was to keep an eye on strangers, and make certain that the disreputable regulars observed some informal but widely understood rules. Drunks and addicts could sit on the stoops, but could not lie down. People could drink on side streets, but not at the main intersection. Bottles had to be in paper bags. Talking to, bothering, or begging from people waiting at the bus stop was strictly forbidden. If a dispute erupted between a businessman and a customer, the businessman was assumed to be right, especially if the customer was a stranger. If a stranger loitered, Kelly would ask him if he had any means of support and what his business was; if he gave unsatisfactory answers, he was sent on his way. Persons who broke the informal rules, especially those who bothered people waiting at bus stops, were arrested for vagrancy. Noisy teenagers were told to keep quiet.

These rules were defined and enforced in collaboration with the "regulars" on the street. Another neighborhood might have different rules, but these, everybody understood, were the rules for *this* neighborhood. If someone violated them, the regulars not only turned to Kelly for help but also ridiculed the violator. Sometimes what Kelly did could be described as "enforcing the law," but just as often it involved taking informal or extralegal steps to help protect what the neighborhood had decided was the appropriate level of public order. Some of the things he did probably would not withstand a legal challenge.

A determined skeptic might acknowledge that a skilled foot-patrol officer can maintain order but still insist that this sort of "order" has little to do with the real sources of community fear—that is, with violent crime. To a degree, that is true. But two things must be borne in mind. First, outside observers should not assume that they know how much of the anxiety now endemic in many big-city neighborhoods stems from a fear of "real" crime and how much from a sense that the street is disorderly, a source of distasteful, worrisome encounters. The people of Newark, to judge from their behavior and their remarks to interviewers, apparently assign a high value to public order, and feel relieved and reassured when the police help them maintain that order.

The Broken Window Theory

Second, at the community level, disorder and crime are usually inextricably linked, in a kind of developmental sequence. Social psychologists and police officers tend to agree that if a window in a building is broken and is left unrepaired, all the rest of the windows will soon be broken. This is as true in nice neighborhoods as in rundown ones. Window-breaking does not necessarily occur on a large scale because some areas are inhabited by determined window-breakers whereas others are populated by window-lovers; rather, one unrepaired broken window is a signal that no one cares, and so breaking more windows costs nothing. (It has always been fun.)

Philip Zimbardo, a Stanford psychologist, reported in 1969 on some experiments testing the broken-window theory. He arranged to have an automobile without license plates parked with its hood up on a street in the Bronx and a comparable automobile on a street in Palo Alto, California. The car in the Bronx was attacked by "vandals" within ten minutes of its "abandonment." The first to arrive were a family—father, mother, and young son—who removed the radiator and battery. Within twenty-four hours, virtually everything of value had been removed. Then random destruction began—windows were smashed, parts torn off, upholstery ripped. Children began to use the car as a playground. Most of the adult "vandals" were well-dressed, apparently clean-cut whites. The car in Palo Alto sat untouched for more than a week. Then Zimbardo smashed part of it with a sledgehammer. Soon, passersby were joining in. Within a few hours, the car had been turned upside down and utterly destroyed. Again, the "vandals" appeared to be primarily respectable whites.

Untended property becomes fair game for people out for fun or plunder and even for people who ordinarily would not dream of doing such things and who probably consider themselves law-abiding. Because of the nature of community life in the Bronx—its anonymity, the frequency with which cars are abandoned and things are stolen or broken, the past experience of "no one caring"—vandalism begins much more quickly than it does in staid Palo Alto, where people have come to believe that private possessions are cared for, and that mischievous behavior is costly. But vandalism can occur anywhere once communal barriers—the sense of mutual regard and the obligations of civility—are lowered by actions that seem to signal that "no one cares."

The Perception of Lawlessness Leads to Crime

We suggest that "untended" behavior also leads to the breakdown of community controls. A stable neighborhood of families who care for their homes, mind each other's children, and confidently frown on unwanted intruders can change, in a few years or even a few months, to an inhospitable and frightening jungle. A piece of property is abandoned, weeds grow up, a window is smashed. Adults stop scolding rowdy children; the children, emboldened, become more rowdy. Families move out, unattached adults move in. Teenagers gather in front of the corner store. The merchant asks them to move; they refuse. Fights occur. Litter accumulates. People start drinking in front of the grocery; in time, an inebriate slumps to the sidewalk and is allowed to sleep it off. Pedestrians are approached by panhandlers.

At this point it is not inevitable that serious crime will flourish or violent attacks on strangers will occur. But many residents will think that crime, especially violent crime, is on the rise, and they will modify their behavior accordingly. They will use the streets less often, and when on the streets will stay apart from their fellows, moving with averted eyes, silent lips, and hurried steps. "Don't get involved." For some residents, this growing atomization will matter little, because the neighborhood is not their "home" but "the place where they live." Their interests are elsewhere; they are cosmopolitans. But it will matter greatly to other people, whose lives derive meaning and satisfaction from local attachments rather than worldly involvement; for them, the neighborhood will cease to exist except for a few reliable friends whom they arrange to meet.

Such an area is vulnerable to criminal invasion. Though it is not inevitable, it is more likely that here, rather than in places where people are confident they can regulate public behavior by informal controls, drugs will change hands, prostitutes will solicit, and cars will be stripped. That the drunks will be robbed by boys who do it as a lark, and the prostitutes' customers will be robbed by men who do it purposefully and perhaps violently. That muggings will occur. . . .

The Role of the Police Officer

The citizen who fears the ill-smelling drunk, the rowdy teenager, or the importuning beggar is not merely expressing his distaste for unseemly behavior; he is also giving voice to a bit of folk wisdom that happens to be a correct generalization—namely, that serious street crime flourishes in areas in which disorderly behavior goes unchecked. The unchecked panhandler is, in effect, the first broken window.

Muggers and robbers, whether opportunistic or professional, believe they reduce their chances of being caught or even identified if they operate on streets where potential victims are already intimidated by prevailing conditions. If the neighborhood cannot keep a bothersome panhandler from annoying passersby, the thief may reason, it is even less likely to call the police to identify a potential mugger or to interfere if the mugging actually takes place.

Some police administrators concede that this process occurs, but argue that motorized-patrol officers can deal with it as effectively as foot-patrol officers. We are not so sure. In theory, an officer in a squad car can observe as much as an officer on foot; in theory, the former can talk to as many people as the latter. But the reality of police-citizen encounters is powerfully altered by the automobile. An officer on foot cannot separate himself from the street people; if he is approached, only his uniform and his personality can help him manage whatever is about to happen. And he can never be certain what that will be—a request for directions, a plea for help, an angry denunciation, a teasing remark, a confused babble, a threatening gesture. . . .

Ordinarily, no judge or jury ever sees the persons caught up in a dispute over the appropriate level of neighborhood order. That is true not only because most cases are handled informally on the street but also because no universal standards are available to settle arguments over disorder, and thus a judge may not be any wiser or more effective than a police officer. Until quite recently in many states, and even today in some places, the police made arrests on such charges as "suspicious person" or "vagrancy" or "public drunkenness"— charges with scarcely any legal meaning. These charges exist not because society wants judges to punish vagrants or drunks but because it wants an officer to have the legal tools to remove undesirable persons from a neighborhood when informal efforts to preserve order in the streets have failed.

The Consequences of Limiting Police Power

Once we begin to think of all aspects of police work as involving the application of universal rules under special procedures, we inevitably ask what constitutes an "undesirable person" and why we should "criminalize" vagrancy or drunkenness. A strong and commendable desire to see that people are treated fairly makes us worry about allowing the police to rout persons who are undesirable by some vague or parochial standard. A growing and not-so-commendable utilitarianism leads us to doubt that any behavior that does not "hurt" another person should be made illegal. And thus many of us who watch over the police are reluctant to allow them to perform, in the only way they can, a function that every neighborhood desperately wants them to perform.

This wish to "decriminalize" disreputable behavior that "harms no one"—and thus remove the ultimate sanction the police can employ to maintain neighborhood order—is, we think, a mistake. Arresting a single drunk or a single vagrant who has harmed no identifiable person seems unjust, and in a sense it is. But failing to do anything about a score of drunks or a hundred vagrants may destroy an entire community. A particular rule that seems to make sense in the individual case makes no sense when it is made a universal rule and applied to all cases. It makes no sense because it fails to take into account the connection between one broken window left untended and a thousand broken windows. Of course, agencies other than the police could attend to the problems posed by drunks or the mentally ill, but in most communities especially where the "deinstitutionalization" movement has been strong—they do not.

The Biological Foundation of Violent Crime

Debra Niehoff

Although the use of insanity as a defence for innocence has existed since ancient Greece and Rome, it was first established in the United States in 1843. Despite the fact that the criteria to establish insanity are more strict in the legal sense than the psychological one, critics have argued that society cannot afford to offer special consideration to those whose crimes were committed under the effects of illnesses such as paranoid schizophrenia, and that this defense has always been open to abuse.

In the following selection, neurobiologist Debra Niehoff examines the role that biology plays in violence. She argues that violent criminal behavior is rarely deterred by the fear of punishment and that a long-term reduction of violence can only be achieved through a combination of behavioral drug therapy, ongoing psychotherapeutic support, and adequate supervision. These three responses are precisely what is lacking in the current penal system, she contends, and that is why the use of prison for punishment of violent offenders has not been effective in reducing crime. In fact, Niehoff argues that incarceration can even exacerbate some conditions such as schizophrenia, making offenders more likely to re-offend on their release. She concludes by arguing that science's growing knowledge of the biological foundations of violence means that accurate diagnosis of conditions such as schizophrenia is possible, and that disallowing the use of the insanity defense for fears of its abuse has had the effect of transforming prisons into unregulated mental institutions.

Debra Niehoff, *The Biology of Violence: How Understanding the Brain, Behavior, and Environment Can Break the Vicious Circle of Aggression*. New York: Free Press, 1999, pp. 259–286.

Crime is down. For six straight years [from 1994–1999], Justice Department statistics show that the rates of murder, rape, armed robbery, and assault have plummeted, to the lowest levels in over a decade. Big-city mayors, police officials, legislators, even the president have congratulated themselves on the success of their anticrime policies. Nevertheless, in 1996, there were still 19,645 murders, 95,769 rapes, over 1 million cases of aggravated assault, and 537,050 robberies amounting to a total loss of nearly $500 million in stolen property.

A woman is sexually assaulted every forty-five seconds. More than one-third of Americans say they have watched a man batter his wife or a girlfriend. Between 1986 and 1993, the number of abused and neglected children doubled, and the number of those seriously injured increased fourfold. According to FBI reports, workplace violence is now our fastest-growing form of murder; in fact, it's second only to traffic accidents as a cause of death on the job. Angry drivers in the throes of road rage kill fifteen hundred people annually, are single-handedly responsible for a steady rise in traffic fatalities over the last four years, and have prompted congressional hearings and the formation of special antiaggression highway patrols. In Philadelphia alone, aggressive "road warriors" injure someone every fifty-seven minutes and kill two to four times more people than drunk drivers do.

We may have made headway with the problem of crime, but we still have a way to go before we've solved the problem of violence.

Getting tough has replaced social reform as the answer to violence. Advocates of longer prison sentences and strict discipline claim that rehabilitation has only led to "revolving-door justice": violent criminals leave prison, commit another crime, return to prison, then repeat the cycle, over and over again, at the public's expense. If we can't seem to change these individuals, they argue, we should give up. Get them off the streets, keep them off as long as possible, and make sure their prison experience is a miserable one. No television, no weightlifting, no college courses, no parole. Teach them a lesson, and make them a public example that will scare potential offenders into putting their guns down.

If the violent really feared punishment, they'd think twice—or would they? We have exiled, imprisoned, burned, maimed, shot, hanged, and electrocuted violent people for centuries, and the killers keep coming. According to Bobbie Huskey, president of the American Correctional Association— the people who run prisons—"our experience shows most offenders don't even think once. They commit crimes on impulse, when they're high or angry, or have no regard for the consequences, and they believe they won't get caught." Punishment will not end violence. The problem keeps coming back; like the sorcerer's apprentice, we march people off to prison, only to find a new generation of violent offenders stepping up to take their place. We discover and prosecute a single act of violence, and a dozen others occur while our attention is diverted.

If we want to make real progress in reducing the level of violence in our society, we have to stop reacting and start thinking. America doesn't need more prisons. We don't lack for resources, programs, people, or character. What we need is a whole new perspective. In place of rhetoric, we need the courage to consider another possibility: that behavior is a dynamic process integrating physiology and experience. If any entity deserves a greater voice in the ongoing debate about violence, it is the brain. . . .

Staying in Line

A world totally devoid of aggression would be biologically unreasonable. Human nature, in the words of ethologist Frans de Waal, is basically good natured; affiliation, not confrontation, guides the overwhelming majority of social interactions. But without the means to protect ourselves and our children, we would be as helpless as plants. Arguments and power plays, as well as displays of affection, are needed to define the social structure, to create the dynamic tension needed to avoid complacency. Provided quarrels do not get out of hand, the result is a more lasting peace.

De Waal emphasizes that "to present all aggression as undesirable, even evil, is like calling all wild plants weeds: it is the perspective of the gardener, not the botanist or ecologist." However, if the protective and organizational dimensions of aggression are to be retained without devolving into destructive violence, it must be contained. Self-control is a more realistic goal than the peaceable kingdom.

Aggression is nature's life insurance. But like your State Farm policy, it's intended to be reserved for life-or-death crises, not cashed out every time you encounter a minor emergency. Controlling aggression requires a nervous system correctly attuned to the demands of the outside world, that recognizes and accepts unambiguous rules, correctly taught. It requires intact executive functions capable of integrating emotional and representational data. It requires a brain unencumbered by disease and uncluttered by interference from recreational drugs.

Violence is the failure to respect the boundary between acceptable and unacceptable aggression. If we want to prevent this breakdown, to have people reserve their strongest responses for true emergencies, we must protect the nervous system from injury, destabilizing levels of stress, drugs, isolation, and victimization. We must strive to create a safe environment where people are not constantly on guard, an environment flexible enough to accommodate some risk taking, structured enough to prevent confusion. And when physiology and environment have conspired to erode control, prompt, decisive action is essential to regaining self-control before it's too late. . . .

Reconstruction, Not Rehabilitation

Rehabilitation is supposed to fix the problems that lead to violent behavior. It can't possibly work, however, if it tries to fix only half of the problem. Job skills are useless if jobs are nonexistent—or if the worker is still too hot-headed to get along with coworkers, too fascinated by alcohol to get to work on time. Counseling isn't a bad idea. But the antisocial don't need a listening ear; they need step-by-step instruction in the mechanics of acceptable social behavior and the incentive to practice these skills. College courses don't cover risk assessment, addiction, or coping with mental illness.

Violent behavior is open to change, but only when *both* the external and internal conditions that have led behavior over the boundary of acceptable force have changed as well. To break the vicious circle between environmental cues, negative perception, and maladaptive behavior, the brain must develop a different attitude toward the outside world, and the world itself must be different. Changing only one side of the equation allows the other to continue to push behavior in the wrong direction. Reconstruction—changing both—establishes a new equilibrium.

Lasting changes in behavior require attention to both physical and environmental elements. Interventions that ignore the neural origins of behavior leave behind a nervous system that's still out of step with the environment, vulnerable to the stress of life or unresponsive to the push and pull of emotion. And the good of interventions that target the brain but ignore environmental forces will soon be undone by the same insults that fueled the destructive dynamic in the first place—especially if the individual has not learned more effective and socially acceptable ways of protecting himself in potentially threatening circumstances.

The key to tempering violent behavior is adjusting the calculation of threat so that the intensity of the response matches the true demand of the situation, without overshooting or undershooting. But how do you rein in a brain that consistently misses the mark? You could do what the brain itself does: take advantage of the unique ability of the frontal cortex to reconsider emotional significance in the light of additional information, to postpone responding until reason, analysis, and insight have had an opportunity to conduct a reality check. . . .

Behavioral Drug Therapy

Medication cannot "cure" violence any more than it can cure heart disease, arthritis, or migraine. But it can limit flare-ups, relieve pain, prevent relapses, and save lives. Used carefully, after proper evaluation, and in conjunction with cognitive therapy or other psychotherapeutic techniques that teach coping and social skills, it does not control people but frees them from behavior that imperils their lives, destroys their relationships with others, and compromises their ability to stay within socially sanctioned boundaries.

We can set guidelines for behavioral drug therapy, just as we can for behavioral genetics, if we are ready to become informed and involved. We can reject coercion, knowing that people will not be helped by drugs they do not want to take. We can insist that research belongs on the outside of prison walls where participants are true volunteers, with the freedom to give truly informed consent and the right to withdraw at any time—and where we have no shortage of violent subjects. But the need for caution does not mean that we cannot design correctional programs that include pharmacotherapy as sentencing options, just as we already recommend drug treatment programs or boot camp.

Thirty-two states have death-penalty laws that authorize execution by lethal injection. If we believe it is acceptable to kill violent individuals with drugs, can we also find it acceptable to save them? . . .

Why Prisons Fail

Our cherished idea that pain deters violence flies in the face of what behavioral biologists know about the relationship between painful experiences and future aggression. In the case of violent behavior, this reasoning is counterproductive. "Punishment is a less desirable method of control, since pain itself is a stimulus to fight," writes pioneer ethologist J.P. Scott. Shock-induced aggression, for all its inadequacies as a model of real-world aggressive behavior, demonstrates conclusively that confinement and pain are highly effective at provoking abnormal aggression. Punitive sentences and strict prison environments may satisfy our desire to "do something," but in the long run, they are unlikely to reduce—in fact, they almost certainly magnify—the risk of violence.

Prisons fail because they rely on procedures that make aggression worse. If we are to continue to depend on incarceration as our first-line defense against violent crime, we must stop using the time spent in prison to perpetuate violence. As Dorothy Otnow Lewis, a pioneer in the study of the relationship between biology and human violence, summed up the problem in an online interview: "Our correctional system reproduces all of the ingredients known to promote violence: isolation, discomfort, pain, exposure to other violent individuals, and general insecurity. In our prisons we have created a laboratory that predictably reproduces and reinforces aggression. Perhaps with a bit of ingenuity we could do the opposite."

Prisons also fail because the people who run them don't understand that *aggression* is a plural noun. As a result, inmates are separated on the basis of age, sex, or estimates of how likely they are to misbehave in prison, not according to the nature of their aggressive behavior. The hostile and the antisocial may be cellmates. Inmates addicted to crack, methamphetamine, heroin—individuals with a nervous system primed to overreact by drugs—are beaten, threatened, sodomized, terrorized, a perfect formula for eliciting an angry retaliation. Predators have an endless source of victims; the chronically mentally ill face an endless series of abusers.

The answer is not more prisons but more detail. Correctional policies can no longer afford to ignore the biological complexity of aggressive behavior. Human violence comes in a range of shapes and sizes. . . . If we were to do only one thing differently, it ought to be interrupting the cycle of violence as early as possible. When more people are pulled out of the system before they are ruined beyond repair, prisons will become what they ought to be: the option of last resort. . . .

Expensive, Cruel and Ineffective

Biology won't make prison obsolete. To disconnect chronically violent individuals from the destructive environments that have contributed to their problem, we often need to remove them physically from these environments. To get their attention, we often need drastic action. But not all violent individuals belong in prison.

People with schizophrenia, for example, are ill-served by incarceration. Imprisoning them may keep them off the streets, but it will not reform them, because they cannot understand that the prison experience is intended to deter repeat offenses. Too confused to defend themselves or read the intentions of others, they are easy prey; victimization only reinforces their perception of threat.

Schizophrenia is not simply an insanity defense. It is not a decision, an act, a state of mind, or a fanciful eccentricity. It is a chronic, incapacitating brain disorder that abolishes rational thinking and turns emotional reactions upside down. Schizophrenics, say experts, do not think the way we do, even when they're not actively hallucinating or delusional. They cannot and typically will not ask for help, because unlike the depressed, the anxious, or the traumatized, they don't recognize that anything is wrong. Whether or not they "know" what they're doing when they commit a violent act, the reason why they're doing it is inevitably bizarre. . . .

Medical Treatment Can Help

The key to containing the unpredictable aggression of the minority of mentally ill individuals who are violent is appropriate medical treatment. The violence of paranoid schizophrenia lies beyond punishment. But it can be effectively controlled with antipsychotic medication, ongoing psychotherapeutic support, and adequate supervision.

Treatment reins in delusional thinking—and fewer delusions mean less need to respond violently to an unseen threat. But treatment measures like medication work only as long as the mentally ill individual remains under their protective influence. If he or she stops taking antipsychotic medication, the risk of violence rapidly escalates. If medical intervention is not to fail as soon as those remanded to treatment are released, mentally ill individuals who have proven to be violent need ongoing supervision, in the form of outpatient commitment, a legally appointed guardian, or a long-term residential community.

Advocates who supported deinstitutionalization and the right to refuse treatment have stripped patients and society alike of the right to safety. The mentally ill, who were supposed to be freed, have been abandoned, at the mercy of threatening delusions that prompt tragic attempts at self-defense. It is time to demand that those who have left the mentally ill to their own devices assume responsibility for the welfare of these patients and that they be held accountable for turning our prisons into mental institutions.

The Internet Has Bred Cyber Crime

Louis J. Freeh

The advent of the Internet in the mid-1990s was accompanied by a variety of technology-based criminal activities collectively known as cyber crime. In the following testimony delivered before the Subcommittee for the Technology, Terrorism, and Government Information of the Senate committee on Judiciary, the director of the Federal Bureau of Investigation, Louis Freeh, examines this burgeoning problem. Principally, cyber crime can be divided into two categories: new forms of criminal behaviour that are internet specific, and the expansion of traditional crimes.

The new forms of technologically-based crime include activites such as hacking and virus writing. While these activities can be profit-motivated, a new form of politically motivated activism known as "hacktivism" has become common. Hacktivists disrupt Web sites and Internet systems in order to send a political message. However, these crimes can also be motiveless insofar as some hackers and virus writers commit their crimes for simple entertainment. While these activities are novel, the widespread use of the Internet has also led to the expansion of traditional crimes. These activities include property theft, fraud, and intellectual property piracy. Freeh also discussed the possibility of technologically sophisticated terrorist groups using the internet to support their operations.

Over the past several years, we have seen a range of computer crimes ranging from defacement of websites by juveniles to sophisticated intrusions that we suspect may be sponsored by foreign powers, and everything in between. Some

Louis J. Freeh, "Statement for the Record of Louis J. Freeh, Director, Federal Bureau of Investigation, on Cybercrime, before the Senate Committee on Judiciary, Subcommittee for the Technology, Terrorism, and Government Information," Washington, DC, March 28, 2000, www.cybercrime.gov.

of these are obviously more significant than others. The theft of national security information from a government agency or the interruption of electrical power to a major metropolitan area have greater consequences for national security, public safety, and the economy than the defacement of a website. But even the less serious categories have real consequences and, ultimately, can undermine confidence in e-commerce and violate privacy or property rights. A website hack that shuts down an e-commerce site can have disastrous consequences for a business. An intrusion that results in the theft of credit card numbers from an online vendor can result in significant financial loss and, more broadly, reduce consumers' willingness to engage in e-commerce. Because of these implications, it is critical that we have in place the programs and resources to investigate and, ultimately, to deter these sorts of crimes.

The following are some of the categories of cyber threats that we confront today.

The Insider

The disgruntled insider (a current or former employee of a company) is a principal source of computer crimes for many companies. Insiders' knowledge of the target companies' network often allows them to gain unrestricted access to cause damage to the system or to steal proprietary data. The just-released 2000 survey by the Computer Security Institute and FBI reports that 71% of respondents detected unauthorized access to systems by insiders.

One example of an insider was George Parente. In 1997, Parente was arrested for causing five network servers at the publishing company Forbes, Inc., to crash. Parente was a former Forbes computer technician who had been terminated from temporary employment. In what appears to have been a vengeful act against the company and his supervisors, Parente dialed into the Forbes computer system from his residence and gained access through a co-worker's log-in and password.

Once online, he caused five of the eight Forbes computer network servers to crash, and erased all of the server volume on each of the affected servers. No data could be restored. Parente's sabotage resulted in a two day shut down in Forbes' New York operations with losses exceeding $100,000. Parente pleaded guilty to one count of violating the Computer Fraud and Abuse Act, Title 18 U.S.C. 1030. . . .

Hackers and "Hacktivism"

Hackers (or "crackers") are also a common threat. They sometimes crack into networks simply for the thrill of the challenge or for bragging rights in the hacker community. Recently, however, we have seen more cases of hacking for illicit financial gain or other malicious purposes.

While remote cracking once required a fair amount of skill or computer knowledge, hackers can now download attack scripts and protocols from the World Wide Web and launch them against victim sites. Thus while attack tools have become more sophisticated, they have also become easier to use. The distributed denial-of-service (DDOS) attacks [in February 2000] are only the most recent illustration of the economic disruption that can be caused by tools now readily available on the Internet.

Another recent case illustrates the scope of the problem. On Friday [March 2000] authorities in Wales [in the UK], acting in coordination with the FBI, arrested two individuals for alleged intrusions into e-commerce sites in several countries and the theft of credit card information on over 26,000 accounts. One subject used the Internet alias "CURADOR." Losses from this case could exceed $3,000,000. The FBI cooperated closely with the Dyfed-Powys Police Service in the United Kingdom, the Royal Canadian Mounted Police in Canada, and private industry. This investigation involved the Philadelphia Division, seven other FBI field offices, our Legal Attache in London, and the NIPC [National Infrastructure

Protection Center]. This case demonstrates the close partnerships that we have built with our foreign law enforcement counterparts and with private industry.

We have also seen a rise recently in politically motivated attacks on web pages or email servers, which some have dubbed "hacktivism." In these incidents, groups and individuals overload e-mail servers or deface web sites to send a political message. While these attacks generally have not altered operating systems or networks, they have disrupted services, caused monetary loss, and denied the public access to websites containing valuable information, thereby infringing on others' rights to disseminate and receive information. Examples of "hacktivism" include a case in 1996, in which an unknown subject gained unauthorized access to the computer system hosting the Department of Justice Internet website. The intruders deleted over 200 directories and their contents on the computer system and installed their own pages. The installed pages were critical of the Communications Decency Act (CDA) and included pictures of Adolf Hitler, swastikas, pictures of sexual bondage scenes, a speech falsely attributed to President Clinton, and a fabricated CDA text.

Virus Writers

Virus writers are posing an increasingly serious threat to networks and systems worldwide. Last year saw the proliferation of several destructive computer viruses or "worms," including the Melissa Macro Virus, the Explore.Zip worm, and the CIH (Chernobyl) Virus. The NIPC frequently sends out warnings or advisories regarding particularly dangerous viruses, which can allow potential victims to take protective steps and minimize the destructive consequences of a virus.

The Melissa Macro Virus was a good example of our twofold response—encompassing both warning and investigation—to a virus spreading in the networks. The NIPC sent out warnings as soon as it had solid information on the virus and its effects; these warnings helped alert the public and re-duce the potential destructive impact of the virus. On the in-vestigative side, the NIPC acted as a central point of contact for the field offices who worked leads on the case. A tip re-ceived by the New Jersey State Police from America Online, and their follow-up investigation with the FBI's Newark Divi-sion, led to the April 1, 1999 arrest of David L. Smith. Mr. Smith pleaded guilty to one count of violating 18 U.S.C. § 1030 in Federal Court, and to four state felony counts. As part of his guilty plea, Smith stipulated to affecting one million computer systems and causing $80 million in damage. . . .

Criminal Groups

We are also seeing the increased use of cyber intrusions by criminal groups who attack systems for purposes of monetary gain. In September 1999, two members of a group dubbed the "Phonemasters" were sentenced after their conviction for theft and possession of unauthorized access devices (18 U.S.C. § 1029) and unauthorized access to a federal interest computer (18 U.S.C. § 1030). The "Phonemasters" were an international group of criminals who penetrated the computer systems of MCI, Sprint, AT&T, Equifax, and even the National Crime In-formation Center. Under judicially approved electronic sur-veillance orders, the FBI's Dallas Division made use of new data intercept technology to monitor the calling activity and modem pulses of one of the suspects, Calvin Cantrell. Mr. Cantrell downloaded thousands of Sprint calling card num-bers, which he sold to a Canadian individual, who passed them on to someone in Ohio. These numbers made their way to an individual in Switzerland and eventually ended up in the hands of organized crime groups in Italy. Cantrell was sentenced to two years as a result of his guilty plea, while one of his associates, Cory Lindsay, was sentenced to 41 months.

The Phonemasters' methods included "dumpster diving" to gather old phone books and technical manuals for systems.

They used this information to trick employees into giving up their login and password information. The group then used this information to break into victims' systems. It is important to remember that often "cyber crimes" are facilitated by old-fashioned guile, such as calling employees and tricking them into giving up passwords. Good cyber-security practices must therefore address personnel security and "social engineering" in addition to instituting electronic security measures. . . .

National Security Threats

Beyond criminal threats in cyber space, we also face a variety of significant national-security threats.

Terrorists groups are increasingly using new information technology and the Internet to formulate plans, raise funds, spread propaganda, and to communicate securely. In his statement on the worldwide threat in 2000, Director of Central Intelligence George Tenet testified that terrorists groups, "including Hizbollah, HAMAS, the Abu Nidal organization, and [Osama] Bin Laden's al Qa'ida organization are using computerized files, e-mail, and encryption to support their operations." In one example, convicted terrorist Ramzi Yousef, the mastermind of the World Trade Center bombing, stored detailed plans to destroy United States airliners on encrypted files on his laptop computer. While we have not yet seen these groups employ cyber tools as a weapon to use against critical infrastructures, their reliance on information technology and acquisition of computer expertise are clear warning signs. Moreover, we have seen other terrorist groups, such as the Internet Black Tigers (who are reportedly affiliated with the Tamil Tigers), engage in attacks on foreign government websites and email servers. "Cyber terrorism"—by which I mean the use of cyber tools to shut down critical national infrastructures (such as energy, transportation, or government operations) for the purpose of coercing or intimidating a government or civilian population—is thus a very real, though still largely potential, threat. . . .

The categories described above involve computers used as weapons and as targets of a crime. We are also seeing computers used to facilitate more traditional forms of crime.

Internet Fraud

One of the most critical challenges facing the FBI and law enforcement in general is the use of the Internet for fraudulent purposes. Understanding and using the Internet to combat Internet fraud is essential for law enforcement. The accessibility of such an immense audience, coupled with the anonymity of the subject, require a different approach. The Internet is a perfect medium to locate victims and provide an environment where victims do not see or speak to the "fraudsters." Anyone in the privacy of their own home can create a very persuasive vehicle for fraud over the Internet. Internet fraud does not have traditional boundaries as seen in the traditional schemes. The traditional methods of detecting, reporting, and investigating fraud fail in this environment. By now it is common knowledge that the Internet is being used to host criminal behavior. The top ten most frequently reported frauds committed on the Internet include Web auctions, Internet services, general merchandise, computer equipment/software, pyramid schemes, business opportunities/franchises, work at home plans, credit card issuing, prizes/sweepstakes, and book sales.

Let me provide you with some specific examples. Securities offered over the Internet have added an entirely new dimension to securities fraud investigations. Investors are able to research potential investments and actually invest over the Internet with ease through electronic linkage to a number of services that provide stock and commodity quotations, as well as, critical financial information. The North American Securities Administrators Association has estimated that Internet-related stock fraud results in an approximately $10 billion per year (or $1 million per hour) loss to investors; this is currently the second most common form of investment fraud. . . .

There is a need for a proactive approach when investigating Internet fraud. There is an essential need to establish a central repository for complaints of Internet fraud. The FBI and the National White Collar Crime Center (NW3C) are addressing this need by cosponsoring the Internet Fraud Complaint Center (IFCC). This partnership will ensure that Internet fraud is addressed at all levels of law enforcement (local, state, and federal). The IFCC is necessary to adequately identify, track, and investigate new fraudulent schemes on the Internet on a national and international level. IFCC personnel will collect, analyze, evaluate, and disseminate Internet fraud complaints to the appropriate law enforcement agency. The IFCC will provide a mechanism by which Internet fraud schemes are identified and addressed through a criminal investigative effort. The IFCC will provide analytical support, and aid in the development of a training module to address Internet fraud. The information obtained from the data collected will provide the foundation for the development of a national strategic plan to address Internet fraud. The IFCC will be open and fully operational on May 8, 2000.

Internet Piracy

Intellectual property is the driver of the 21st century American economy. In many ways it has become what America does best. The United States is the leader in the development of creative, technical intellectual property. Violations of Intellectual Property Rights [IPR], therefore, threaten the very basis of our economy. Of primary concern is the development and production of trade secret information. The American Society of Industrial Security estimated the potential losses at $2 billion per month in 1997. Pirated products threaten public safety in that many are manufactured to inferior or nonexistent quality standards. A growing percentage of IPR violations now involve the Internet. There are thousands of web sites solely devoted to the distribution of pirated materials. The FBI has recognized, along with other federal agencies, that a coordinated effort must be made to attack this problem. The FBI, along with the Department of Justice, U.S. Customs Service, and other agencies with IPR responsibilities, will be opening an IPR Center this year to enhance our national ability to investigate and prosecute IPR crimes through the sharing of information among agencies. . . .

The Legal Landscape

To deal with this crime problem, we must look at whether changes to the legal procedures governing investigation and prosecution of cyber crimes are warranted. The problem of Internet crime has grown at such a rapid pace that the laws have not kept up with the technology. The FBI is working with the Department of Justice to propose a legislative package for your review to help keep our laws in step with these advances.

One example of some of the problems law enforcement is facing is the jurisdictional limitation of pen registers and trap-and-trace orders issued by federal district courts. These orders allow only the capturing of tracing information, not the content of communications. Currently, in order to track back a hacking episode in which a single communication is purposely routed through a number of Internet Service Providers that are located in different states, we generally have to get multiple court orders. This is because, under current law, a federal court can order communications carriers only within its district to provide tracing information to law enforcement. As a result of the fact that investigators typically have to apply for numerous court orders to trace a single communication, there is a needless waste of time and resources, and a number of important investigations are either hampered or derailed entirely in those instances where law enforcement gets to a communications carrier after that carrier has already discarded the necessary information. For example, [infamous hacker] Kevin Mitnick evaded attempts to trace his calls by moving around the country and by using cellular phones, which routed calls through multiple carriers on their way to the final destination. It was impossible to get orders quickly enough in all the jurisdictions to trace the calls. . . .

With regards to additional legal mechanisms needed by law enforcement to help maintain our abilities to obtain usable evidence in an encrypted world, [in] September [1999] the [Clinton] Administration announced a "New Approach to Encryption." This new approach included significant changes to the nation's encryption export policies and, more importantly, recommended public safety enhancement to ensure "that law enforcement has the legal tools, personnel, and equipment necessary to investigate crime in an encrypted world." . . .

Finally, we should consider whether current sentencing provisions for computer crimes provide an adequate deterrence. Given the degree of harm that can be caused by a virus, intrusion, or a denial of service—in terms of monetary loss to business and consumers, infringement of privacy, or threats to public safety when critical infrastructures are affected it would be appropriate to consider . . . whether penalties established years ago remain adequate.

Examining the Connections Between Ethnicity and Crime

T.L. Meares

It has long been noted that the ethnic composition of the U.S. prison population does not correspond to that of the larger population. African Americans, Native Americans, and Hispanics make up a disproportionately high percentage of those incarcerated. The racial disparities of the justice system are not, however, unique to America. For example, France incarcerates a disproportionate number of Muslim Moroccans, while Canada's prisons house a significantly higher percentage of First Nations people. Indeed, minority groups in every Western country are likely to be imprisoned in disproportionate numbers.

In the following selection professor of law T.L. Meares examines the relationship between ethnicity and crime in an effort to understand why some minority groups are overrepresented in the justice system. She concludes that there are two reasons for this disparity: discrimination by the criminal justice system and disproportionate offending by minority groups. Of the first, she argues that police tactics are more likely to uncover minority offending in the first place, and that the court further discriminates in its sentencing decisions. Although systematic discrimination accounts for some of the racial disparity in incarceration rates, there is also the question of disproportionate offending. There are many theories as to why certain minority groups commit more crime. Meares considers the main theories but finds each lacking in its ability to fully understand the relationship between ethnic minorities and crime.

T.L. Meares, "Crime and Ethnicity (Including Race)," *International Encyclopedia of the Social & Behavioral Sciences*. Oxford: Elsevier, 2001. pp. 2914–18. Copyright © 2001 Elsevier Science Ltd. All rights reserved. Reproduced with permission from Elsevier.

The term 'race' once referred to the 'major biological divisions of mankind' (Caucasoid, Negroid, and Mongoloid), as characterized by skin color, hair texture, and other physical features. . . . This notion has fallen into disrepute for lack of scientific validation. Race is now recognized as a social construct used by groups seeking to delineate themselves from others. Ethnicity is a similar concept that principally refers to the countries from which an individual's heritage can be traced (e.g., 'Hispanic' refers to those with Spanish ancestry), although it is also associated with language, religion, cultural practices, and self-perception. The meanings of these terms continue to be debated, and usage is not consistent internationally. . . .

Crime typically is defined as 'a social harm that the law makes punishable'. . . . Examples of crime range from white-collar crimes and organized crime, to murder and hate crimes. This [selection] will focus on conduct often referred to as 'street-crime' (also known in the US as Index Crime: murder and nonnegligent manslaughter, forcible rape, robbery, burglary, aggravated assault, larceny-theft, motor vehicle theft, and arson), because current records provide the best data for analysis of variation in offending and victimization by race and ethnicity. . . .

Minorities and Incarceration

[Professor of criminal law Michael] Tonry . . . notes that 'members of *some* disadvantaged minority groups in every Western country are disproportionately likely to be arrested, convicted, and imprisoned for violent, property, and drug crimes.' Whether or not this is a more universal phenomenon is as yet unknown, as research has largely been limited to English-speaking and European countries. Regardless, what is now known is disturbing enough. Racial disparities in arrest and incarceration have historically been of particular concern to researchers in the US, and it is with that data that this investigation begins.

The Federal Bureau of Investigation (FBI) has collected crime data since 1930 and annually produces the Uniform Crime Report (UCR). The UCR details arrest data for four racial groups (White, Black, Native American, and Asian), but it does *not* include ethnicity. These data are necessarily incomplete, as they only reflect crimes reported to the police, yet they reveal the stubborn stability of racial disproportion in US arrestees for Index crimes. . . .

In 1996, African Americans were arrested at a rate disproportionate to their representation in the general population ranging from 1.9 times for arson to 4.6 times for robbery.

Research indicates racial and ethnic disparities in US jail and prison populations as well. In 1990, 14 percent of jail inmates were Hispanics, who composed only 9 percent of the general population. More notable is the fact that in 1992, 27 percent of federal prison inmates were Hispanic. US jail and prison data revealed that in 1990, 47 and 51 percent of each population was African American, respectively; the percentage of African American prison intimates has exhibited an upward trend since the 1920s. In 1997, 1,083 of every 100,000 American Indians were in jail—the highest rate for any race.

The US is not alone in exhibiting racial and ethnic disparity in arrests and imprisonment. Australian records, for example, indicate disparity in the arrest of Aborigines—considered a racial minority in that country. Aborigines were almost 8 times more likely to be arrested than non-Aborigines in 1990; the rate increased to 9.2 by 1994. Additional data show that Aboriginal juveniles particularly are likely to be arrested or detained. Data from 1993 reveal ethnic or racial disparities in the prisons of England, Wales, and Canada. Blacks (people of West Indian, Guyanese, and African origin) represented 11 percent of the male English and Welsh prison population, while comprising only 1.8 percent of the young adult males in the general population. Aggregating across all Canadian provinces, researchers found that in 1993–1994, when about 3.7

percent of the Canadian general population was Aboriginal, Aborigines composed 17 percent of provincial prison admittees. Blacks are also over-represented. Data from Ontario correctional facilities reveal a prison admission rate of 705 per 100,000 for whites, 1,992 per 100,000 for Aboriginals, and 3,686 per 100,000 for Blacks.

Notably, while *some* minorities are overrepresented in various criminal justice systems, others are underrepresented, either in the aggregate or in arrest rates for specific offenses. In England, the rates of imprisonment among Indians, Pakistanis, and Bangladeshis are generally *lower* than that of whites, despite their generally poorer economic position. Likewise, a 1992 profile of US prison populations showed that Asians were underrepresented. Asians comprised 3 percent of the general population, yet they made up only about half of one percent of state inmates and just over 1 percent of federal inmates.

Thus, minorities are over and underrepresented in Western justice systems—usually the former. Why?

Evidence of Discrimination

The debate concerning minority overrepresentation in justice system processing has largely centered around two questions. Are racial and ethnic disparities the result of discrimination by criminal justice system actors? Or are they the result of disproportionate offending? Current research strongly suggests that racial and ethnic disproportionate representation in international justice systems results from both factors.

The evidence does *not* suggest that bias is systematic: it does not afflict Western justice systems at all levels, in all cases, and at all times. Rather, it suggests that in certain cases, places, and times, minorities are more likely than majority members to face discrimination in interactions with justice system components. Four arenas evidencing bias are worth discussing briefly: 'Neutral' processes, police practices, drug law enforcement, and the death penalty.

Research has confirmed that two practices, designed to be 'race neutral' in implementation, operate to the disadvantage of minorities on a regular basis: pretrial detention, and plea-bargaining. Though it seems logical to hold before trial those most likely to flee, international scholars have discovered that the characteristics associated with flight risk are more likely to be present in the minority population than in the majority, which results in racial disparities in pretrial detention. Similarly, minorities are less likely to plead guilty. Research indicates that this tendency is shaped by and contributes to the beliefs many minorities have about justice system bias.

Police Practices

The first experience many minorities have with the criminal justice system comes through contact with the police. The police function entails vast enforcement discretion, so the possibility of abuse of authority is ever-present. In the countries in which minorities are overrepresented in the justice system, there is also minority dissatisfaction with police practices. Reports of brutality and unnecessary stops, searches, and arrests fuel these views. In a 1994 US study, 47 percent of African Americans surveyed reported having been harassed by police, while only 10 percent of Whites reported harassment. Researchers in Maryland found that African Americans were the subject of 77 percent of vehicle searches conducted by state troopers in 1995; no contraband was found in 67 percent of the cases. Similarly, the police forces of Glasgow, London, Ottawa, and Toronto are among those who have come under scrutiny recently.

It is possible that police practices impacting primarily minorities also affect the opinions of the police held by the majority population. In a survey conducted in 1981 and 1990 in 20 countries, only a minority of *all* citizens polled, ranging from a high of about 40 percent in Britain to a low nearing 5 percent in Argentina, expressed 'a great deal' of confidence in their nation's police; in all but four of these countries the percentage had *declined* by 1990.

Drug Enforcement

Since the 1980s, the problem of race, ethnicity, and crime in the US and elsewhere has been driven by drug laws and policies that have resulted in the rapid rise in the incarceration rate of minorities. The increase in the Black prison population in the US, England, and Wales is obviously tied to drug law violations. In these countries minorities tend to be convicted of relatively low-level drug offenses at rates much higher than those of the majority of individuals. Scholars have concluded that the stark racial disparities in arrests and incarceration resulting from drug law enforcement are difficult to justify given the small gains in crime control from these policies. . . .

Death Penalty

This issue is of particular concern to scholars in the US, as it is the only Western democracy still imposing this sentence. Examination of sentencing practices indicates that the *victim's* race, not the offender's, most often determines whether or not the defendant will receive the death penalty. Those who murder Whites are more likely to receive the death penalty than those who murder Blacks. African American defendants charged with murdering Whites are most likely to receive the ultimate sanction.

Despite this evidence, the US Supreme Court has refused to void the death penalty, finding in *McCleskey v. Kemp* (1987) that defendants must demonstrate, in addition to discriminatory effect, that the prosecutor's decision to pursue the death penalty in a particular case was the result of racial animus. Today, US death rows are still predominantly minority. Not one death row defendant has yet been able to demonstrate the evidentiary requirements stipulated by *McCleskey*. . . .

Why do Minorities Disproportionately Offend?

Minority groups overrepresented in justice systems tend to be economically and socially disadvantaged, especially compared to the majority. In many cases this is the result of historical discrimination, or is tied to the group's recent immigration to their new national home. Often racial and ethnic minority groups are segregated geographically from other groups. *Social disorganization theory* postulates that the geographical concentration of poverty, along with factors such as joblessness and family disruption, negatively impacts the ability of community-level institutions to mediate crime. . . . This theory helps to explain why some disproportionately minority areas—especially urban ones—exhibit high crime rates. But it does not explain why particular individuals do or do not engage in crime. It is primarily for this reason that attempts to incorporate the notion of 'rotten social background' as a legal excuse for crime commission have been unsuccessful.

Other explanations for minority involvement in the criminal justice system emphasize power and social relationships over economic disadvantage. *Conflict theory* suggests that discriminatory justice practices are simply another expression of the disproportionate power distribution in society. The dominant group can and does use available means to maintain its grip on power. . . . *Cultural conflict theory* maintains that heterogeneous societies tend toward disparate values and are thus more vulnerable to crime. . . . This theory suggests that some minority groups, for various reasons, do not accept majority values, increasing the likelihood of criminal behavior. Finally, *social strain theory* sees increased criminality as one of several responses to the tension inherent in a society in which many lack the means to obtain dominant goals in the generally agreed upon manner. . . . Rebellion and retreatism (e.g., through drug use) are among the other reactions to this type of societal stress. While each of these theories has certain merits, none does a particularly good job of explaining why some disadvantaged minorities are disproportionately *underrepresented* in criminal justice systems.

Drug Abuse Causes Crime

David Boyum and Mark A.R. Kleiman

Drugs have often been associated with crime. In part this is because the possession or use of many drugs has been made illegal, thereby forcing drug users to participate in an illicit market which in itself produces further crimes. If this were the only connection between drugs and crime, then the decriminalization of drugs would certainly result in a massive reduction of drug-related crime. However, independent public-policy consultant David Boyum and Professor of Public Policy Mark A.R. Kleiman argue in the following viewpoint that drugs and crime are linked in three other important ways. The first link is the result of the behavioral effects of drug use, which weaken self control and increase lawbreaking activities. The second link is the addicts' need for money to supply their habits, which often results in crimes such as theft. The third connection between drugs and crime is that the illegal nature of the business invites violent crime between dealers competing for territory.

Boyum and Kleiman analyze drug-enforcement policies and find that the law is ill equipped to combat drug-related crime and can even exacerbate the problem. The authors propose an alternative and controversial policy which they term "testing and sanctions." They argue that the only way to reduce drug crimes is to force drug-using offenders to stop using drugs, or in the authors' words, the law must "mandate desistence." They propose a system whereby felons are obligated to undergo regular drug testing, and, if found using, punished. Boyum and Kleiman insist that the benefits of such a system would be the reduction of drug-related crime, the identification of those whose addiction required treatment, and the disruption of the drug market.

David Boyum and Mark A.R. Kleiman, "Breaking the Drug-Crime Link," *The Public Interest*, no. 152, Summer 2003, pp. 19–38. Copyright © 2003 by National Affairs, Inc. Reproduced by permission of the authors.

The American criminal justice system now spends a significant proportion of its resources enforcing the drug laws.
[In 2003] more than 10 percent of all arrests and about 20
percent of all incarcerations involve drug law violations. (Most
of the 1.5 million annual drug arrests are for simple possession, while the majority of the 325,000 people behind bars on
drug charges are there for dealing.) Drug-related arrests are
up 50 percent [since 1993], and drug-related incarceration is
up 80 percent. And the burden of drug law enforcement falls
especially on urban minority communities: Will Brownsberger
and Anee Morrison Piehl of Harvard found that the poorest
neighborhoods in Massachusetts, with a little more than 10
percent of the state's population, accounted for 57 percent of
state prison commitments for drug offenses, while [professor
of public policy and criminology] Peter Reuter and his colleagues at RAND [an American think tank] estimated that
nearly a third of African-American males born in the District
of Columbia in the 1960s were charged with selling drugs between the ages of 18 and 24.

Such vigorous enforcement of drug prohibition, while
controversial, enjoys substantial support. This is partly because drug laws are seen as protecting people—especially, but
not exclusively, children—from drug abuse and addiction. But
it is also because drug prohibition and enforcement are widely
believed to prevent burglary, robbery, assault, and other predatory crime, a view apparently born out by the violence that
surrounds much drug dealing and the high rates of drug use
among active criminals. Because drug trafficking is inherently
violent and because illicit drug use is a catalyst for criminal
behavior, the argument goes, enforcement efforts to suppress
drug selling and drug taking will tend to reduce crime. . . .

Intoxication and Crime

Intoxication and addiction, in certain circumstances, appear to
encourage careless and combative behavior. The key empirical

observation here is that more crimes—and, in particular, more violent crimes—are committed under the the influence of alcohol than under the influence of all illegal drugs combined. When state and federal prisoners were asked about the circumstances of the offences that landed them in prison, 24 percent said they were under the influence of illicit drugs (but not alcohol) at the time, 30 percent cited intoxication with alcohol alone, and 17 percent named drugs and alcohol together. That alcohol, a legal and inexpensive drug, is implicated in so much crime suggests that substance abuse itself, and not just economic motivation or the perverse effects of illicit markets, can play a significant role in crime.

This connection is hardly surprising. Anything that weakens self-control and reduces foresight is likely to increase lawbreaking activities. Most crime doesn't pay, and being high is one good way to forget that fact. (Driving drunk, for example, rarely stands up to cost-benefit analysis from the drunk driver's viewpoint, yet many otherwise sensible people engage in it.) Some forms of intoxication also make certain crimes seem more rewarding, as well as making punishments seem less threatening. And most of us know people who become aggressive when drunk or high.

However, the immediate effects of intoxication are not the only, or necessarily the most significant, connection between drug taking and crime. Chronic intoxication impairs school and job performance, makes its victims less able to delay gratification, and damages relationships with friends and family. All of these tend to increase criminality.

Drugs, Cash, and Violence

The second important link between drugs and crime involves drug users' need for large amounts of quick cash due to the high costs of maintaining an illegal drug habit. The average heavy heroin or cocaine user consumes about $10,000 to $15,000 worth of drugs per year, a sum that most of them cannot generate legally. In one survey of convicted inmates, 39 percent of cocaine and crack users claimed to have committed their current offense in order to get money to buy drugs.

Nonetheless, the economic links between drug use and income-generating crime go both ways. Drug users commit crimes to obtain drug money—in part because their drug use reduces opportunities for legitimate work—but there is also the "paycheck effect." Just as some heavy drinkers splurge at the local bar on payday, drug-involved offenders may buy drugs because crime gives them the money to do so. Thus income-generating crime may lead to drug use, as well as the other way around.

The drug trade provides the third connection between drugs and crime. Because selling drugs is illegal, business arrangements among dealers cannot be enforced by law. Consequently, territorial disputes among dealers, employer-employee disagreements, and arguments over the price, quantity, and quality of drugs are all subject to settlement by force. Since dealers have an incentive to be at least as well-armed as their competitors, violent encounters among dealers, or between a dealer and a customer, often prove deadly. . . .

Enforcement Policies

Drug control policies are typically categorized into enforcement, prevention, and treatment. Enforcement is the dominant activity of American drug policy. Domestic law enforcement accounts for about half of the federal drug control budget; including state and local activity; enforcement's share is about three-quarters of total drug control spending.

Until recently, academic analyses of drug enforcement and crime viewed the price of drugs as a key factor. That analysis turned out to be wrong on two accounts. First, it was assumed that tougher enforcement could substantially increase the price of drugs. The theory was that when enforcement threatened drug traffickers and dealers with the risks of arrest, imprisonment, and the loss of their drugs, money, and physical assets, sellers would charge higher prices as compensation for those risks. It was also assumed that the demand for drugs was, in the short run, relatively unresponsive to price ("inelastic," in economics terminology), meaning that an enforcement-led price increase would result in greater total expenditures on drugs. The implications of these assumptions were that enforcement would indirectly lead users to commit more crimes for drug money, and that market-related violence would also rise, as dealers battled over a larger revenue pool. It was in principle possible that the fall in abuse-related crime stemming from slightly reduced consumption would be greater than the combined increases in crimes committed by dealers seeking competitive advantage and by users looking for drug money. But the arithmetic of relatively inelastic demand (again, in the short run) was discouraging. (In the long run, higher prices tend to reduce the incidence of addiction and increase the rate of recovery, thus reducing crime.)

Today, these underlying assumptions look shaky. Recent research indicates that the demand for cocaine and heroin is far more responsive to price than previously assumed, so much so that the old critique of drug law enforcement as counterproductive in terms of predatory crime seems to have been mistaken. If we remained confident that more, or better, drug law enforcement could substantially raise prices, boosting such enforcement in the cocaine and heroin markets would now appear to be an effective, and perhaps cost effective, crime control measure.

However, confidence in the ability of enforcement to raise prices has been slipping, even as appreciation of the value of such price increases has been growing. [Since the 1980s], a dramatic increase in enforcement efforts has been accompanied by an equally dramatic drop in cocaine and heroin prices. In the 1990s, for example, the number of incarcerated drug offenders roughly doubled, while inflation-adjusted cocaine and heroin prices fell by half. Why cocaine and heroin prices have fallen in the face of increased punishment for drug law violations is something of a puzzle, but the easy replacement of dealers who have been removed from the drug trade is surely part of the explanation.

Suppose that a drug dealer is arrested and imprisoned. That, in effect, creates a job opening for a new dealer. When the first dealer it released from prison and, as is likely, reenters the drug trade, there are now two dealers where once there was one. Writ large, this story suggests that conventional drug enforcement, by imprisoning hundreds of thousands of dealers and thereby drawing hundreds of thousands of others into the drug trade, may significantly increase the long-run supply of dealers. The logical result is downward pressure on prices. . . .

Prevention programs, aimed at reducing experimentation and occasional use primarily by children and adolescents, enjoy strong support across the political spectrum. Even modestly successful prevention programs are unambiguously beneficial in reducing crime. They offer the benefit of reduced drug use and reduced drug dealing without any of the unwanted side-effects of enforcement.

That's the good news about prevention. The bad news is that few prevention programs have demonstrated that they can consistently reduce the number of their subjects who use drugs. . . .

An Alternative: Testing and Sanctions

Several factors limit the capacity of drug treatment, whether voluntary or coerced, to reduce crime. These include the limited availability of treatment, deficiencies in technique and quality, the reluctance of many drug-involved offenders to undergo treatment, and the administrative and procedural difficulties of coerced treatment. It is commonly thought that the limits on treatment are also the limits on the criminal justice system's ability to influence the drug taking of those under its jurisdiction. This view, however, assumes that most users of expensive illicit drugs suffer from clinically diagnosable substance-abuse or dependency disorders, that they have no volitional control over their drug taking, and that all such disorders are invariably chronic and go into remission only with professional intervention. Happily, not one of these propositions is true.

Many users, even frequent users, of cocaine, heroin, and methamphetamine do not meet clinical criteria for substance abuse or dependency. ("Substance abuse" as a legal matter merely means use of a prohibited drug, or use of a prescription drug for nonmedical reasons or without a valid prescription; "substance abuse" as a medical matter is defined by criteria such as escalation of dosage and frequency, narrowing of the behavioral repertoire, loss of control over use, and continued use despite adverse consequences.) Even for those who do meet these clinical criteria, actual consumption is not a constant but rather varies with the availability of the drug and the consequences, especially the more-or-less immediate consequences, of taking it. Incentives influence drug use, even within the treatment context. Monitoring drug use by urine testing enhances treatment outcomes, as does the provision of even very small rewards for compliance. Moreover, while the minority of substance-abusing or substance-dependent individuals who suffer from chronic forms of those disorders makes up a large proportion of the population in treatment, the most common pattern of substance abuse is a single active period followed by "spontaneous" (i.e., not treatment-mediated) remission.

All this being the case, persuading or forcing drug-using offenders into treatment is not the only way to reduce their drug consumption. An alternative to requiring treatment is to mandate desistance from the use of illicit drugs for persons on probation, parole, or pretrial release. Desistance can be enforced by frequent drug tests, with predictable and nearly immediate sanctions for each missed test or incident of detected drug use. While in the long term drug-involved offenders who remain drug-involved are likely to be rearrested and eventually incarcerated, those long-term and probabilistic threats, even if the penalties involved are severe, may be less effective than short-term, but more certain, sanctions.

For those offenders whose drug use is subject to their volitional control, testing-and-sanctions programs can reduce the frequency of drug use. Those unable to control themselves, even under threat, will be quickly identified, and in a way that is likely to break through the denial that often characterizes substance-abuse disorders. Identifying these persons will enable the system to direct treatment resources to those most in need of them. It will also help create a "therapeutic alliance" between treatment providers and clients by giving clients strong incentives to succeed, as opposed merely to wanting the therapists off their backs.

Since recent arrestees account for most of the cocaine and heroin sold in the United States, and therefore for most of the revenues of the illicit markets, an effective testing-and-sanctions program would have a larger impact on the volume of the illicit trade—and presumably on the side-effects it generates, including the need for drug law enforcement and related imprisonment—than any other initiative that could be undertaken. By one estimate, a national program of this type could reasonably be expected to shrink total hard-drug volumes by 40 percent.

CHAPTER 2

Preventing Crime

Chapter Preface

Deterrence has long been one of society's main tools in the prevention of crime. Uniformed police officers are meant not only to apprehend suspects once a crime has been committed but also to serve as symbols to discourage would-be lawbreakers. The first professional police force did not exist in America until 1838, when Boston organized an independent, around-the-clock force. Prior to this time crime prevention was the responsibility of each member of the community. This system of community policing worked well so long as communities remained small; with the advent of towns, an official representative of the state, generally a sheriff, was appointed to uphold the law. With the development of cities, the sheriff's ability to organize posses of private citizens to apprehend criminals was no longer deemed effective and professional police forces were established.

Of course, the fear of being apprehended by law enforcement works as a deterrent for criminal behavior insofar as it leads to punishment. Punishment in colonial America regularly involved public shaming, either by a public whipping or by locking the prisoner in a wooden framework in the town square. Imprisonment, however, was rarely used as a form of punishment. Jails were generally used for persons awaiting trial, for debtors, and sometimes for witnesses. Following the American Revolution, reformers began to argue that criminals should not face corporal punishment but should instead serve sentences in prisons. Principally, reformers argued that prisons were a more effective deterrent to crime as they not only removed the criminal from society but also could reform criminal behavior through incarceration, hard labor, and penitence.

It would be tempting to think that, 150 years after the introduction of an organized police force and the advent of the modern prison system, criminologists could report with some certainty on the effectiveness of the legal system as a deterrent to crime. Yet criminologists continue to debate the effectiveness of various deterrents. While many intuitively believe that a greater police presence reduces crime, others have used statistics to argue otherwise. Still others argue that what is needed is a return to the type of community policing evident in colonial America, whereby an armed citizenry takes responsibility for upholding the law. Though some argue that tough laws and long prison sentences result in less crime, others argue that they do not have a significant deterrent effect on habitual criminals, who are responsible for the majority of crime.

Further complicating the problem of crime deterrence is the issue of civil rights. Get-tough-on-crime measures invariably have a negative effect on the civil rights that are the privileges of liberty guaranteed by law. Such rights include the right to privacy, freedom of movement, and the right to bear arms. While it may be possible to prevent more crime by expanding police powers to allow the search of a suspect's home without a warrant based on probable cause, it would represent such an intolerable violation of civil liberties that its deterrence value would be lost amid civil rights challenges. Thus, all strategies for the prevention of crime must be considered not only for their ability to reduce crime but also for their effect on the everyday lives of law-abiding citizens.

America Declares a War on Drugs

Richard Nixon

In the following speech, delivered before Congress on June 17, 1971, President Richard Nixon declares a "full-scale attack on the problem of drug abuse in America." Nixon argues that existing narcotics legislation is not sufficient to deal with the problem of drug abuse and that what is needed is a comprehensive effort that deals with the various facets of the illegal drug trade. Traditionally, the government had focused its efforts on the prosecution of drug dealers, but Nixon observes that this approach neglects to address the laws of supply and demand that fuel the business of narcotics. In order to combat the problems produced by the drug trade, he argues that the government must attempt to rehabilitate current drug addicts in order to lessen the demand, as well as attack drug traffickers so as to lessen the supply. Amongst his new initiatives are research projects for the development of techniques for detecting drug users, the development of herbicides that target narcotics-producing plants, an increased number of officials charged with apprehending those that break narcotics laws, and the stated intention to combat the international production of drugs.

In New York City more people between the ages of fifteen and thirty-five years die as a result of narcotics than from any other single cause.

In 1960, less than 200 narcotic deaths were recorded in New York City. In 1970, the figure had risen to over 1,000. These statistics do not reflect a problem indigenous to New York City. Although New York is the one major city in the Na-

Richard Nixon, "Special Message to the Congress on Drug Abuse Prevention and Control, June 17, 1971," *Public Papers of the Presidents of the United States: Richard Nixon.* Washington D.C.: U.S. Government Printing Office, 1972, pp. 739–49.

tion which has kept good statistics on drug addiction, the problem is national and international. We are moving to deal with it on both levels.

As part of this administration's ongoing efforts to stem the tide of drug abuse which has swept America in the last decade, we submitted legislation in July of 1969 for a comprehensive reform of Federal drug enforcement laws. Fifteen months later, in October, 1970, the Congress passed this vitally-needed legislation, and it is now producing excellent results. Nevertheless, in the fifteen months between the submission of that legislation and its passage, much valuable time was lost.

We must now candidly recognize that the deliberate procedures embodied in present efforts to control drug abuse are not sufficient in themselves. The problem has assumed the dimensions of a national emergency. I intend to take every step necessary to deal with this emergency, including asking the Congress for an amendment to my 1972 budget to provide an additional $155 million to carry out these steps. This will provide a total of $371 million for programs to control drug abuse in America.

A New Approach to Rehabilitation

While experience thus far indicates that the enforcement provisions of the Comprehensive Drug Abuse Prevention and Control Act of 1970 are effective, they are not sufficient in themselves to eliminate drug abuse. Enforcement must be coupled with a rational approach to the reclamation of the drug user himself. The laws of supply and demand function in the illegal drug business as in any other. We are taking steps under the Comprehensive Drug Act to deal with the supply side of the equation and I am recommending additional steps to be taken now. But we must also deal with demand. We must rehabilitate the drug user if we are to eliminate drug abuse and all the antisocial activities that flow from drug abuse.

Narcotic addiction is a major contributor to crime. The cost of supplying a narcotic habit can run from $30 a day to $100 a day. This is $210 to $700 a week, or $10,000 a year to over $36,000 a year. Untreated narcotic addicts do not ordinarily hold jobs. Instead, they often turn to shoplifting, mugging, burglary, armed robbery, and so on. They also support themselves by starting other people—young people—on drugs. The financial costs of addiction are more than $2 billion every year, but these costs can at least be measured. The human costs cannot. American society should not be required to bear either cost.

Despite the fact that drug addiction destroys lives, destroys families, and destroys communities, we are still not moving fast enough to meet the problem in an effective way. Our efforts are strained through the Federal bureaucracy. Of those we can reach at all under the present Federal system—and the number is relatively small—of those we try to help and who want help, we cure only a tragically small percentage.

A Full-Scale Attack

Despite the magnitude of the problem, despite our very limited success in meeting it, and despite the common recognition of both circumstances, we nevertheless have thus far failed to develop a concerted effort to find a better solution to this increasingly grave threat. At present, there are nine Federal agencies involved in one fashion or another with the problem of drug addiction. There are anti-drug abuse efforts in Federal programs ranging from vocational rehabilitation to highway safety. In this manner our efforts have been fragmented through competing priorities, lack of communication, multiple authority, and limited and dispersed resources. The magnitude and the severity of the present threat will no longer permit this piecemeal and bureaucratically-dispersed effort at drug control. If we cannot destroy the drug menace in America, then it will surely in time destroy us. I am not prepared to accept this alternative.

Therefore, I am transmitting legislation to the Congress to consolidate at the highest level a full-scale attack on the problem of drug abuse in America. I am proposing the appropriation of additional funds to meet the cost of rehabilitating drug users, and I will ask for additional funds to increase our enforcement efforts to further tighten the noose around the necks of drug peddlers, and thereby loosen the noose around the necks of drug users.

At the same time I am proposing additional steps to strike at the "supply" side of the drug equation—to halt the drug traffic by striking at the illegal producers of drugs, the growing of those plants from which drugs are derived, and trafficking in these drugs beyond our borders.

America has the largest number of heroin addicts of any nation in the world. And yet, America does not grow opium—of which heroin is a derivative—nor does it manufacture heroin, which is a laboratory process carried out abroad. This deadly poison in the American lifestream is, in other words, a foreign import. In the last year, heroin seizures by Federal agencies surpassed the total seized in the previous ten years. Nevertheless, it is estimated that we are stopping less than 20 percent of the drugs aimed at this Nation. No serious attack on our national drug problem can ignore the international implications of such an effort, nor can the domestic effort succeed without attacking the problem on an international plane. I intend to do that. . . .

A Coordinated Federal Response

A large number of Federal Government agencies are involved in efforts to fight the drug problem either with new programs or by expanding existing programs. Many of these programs are still experimental in nature. This is appropriate. The problems of drug abuse must be faced on many fronts at the same time, and we do not yet know which efforts will be most successful. But we must recognize that piecemeal efforts, even where individually successful, cannot have a major impact on the drug abuse problem unless and until they are forged together into a broader and more integrated program involving all levels of government and private effort. We need a coordinated effort if we are to move effectively against drug abuse.

The magnitude of the problem, the national and international implications of the problem, and the limited capacities of States and cities to deal with the problem all reinforce the conclusion that coordination of this effort must take place at the highest levels of the Federal Government.

Therefore, I propose the establishment of a central authority with overall responsibility for all major Federal drug abuse prevention, education, treatment, rehabilitation, training, and research programs in all Federal agencies. This authority would be known as the Special Action Office of Drug Abuse Prevention. It would be located within the Executive Office of the President and would be headed by a Director accountable to the President. Because this is an emergency response to a national problem which we intend to bring under control, the Office would be established to operate only for a period of three years from its date of enactment, and the President would have the option of extending its life for an additional two years if desirable.

This Office would provide strengthened Federal leadership in finding solutions to drug abuse problems. It would establish priorities and instill a sense of urgency in Federal and federally-supported drug abuse programs, and it would increase coordination between Federal, State, and local rehabilitation efforts. . . .

Rehabilitation: A New Priority

When traffic in narcotics is no longer profitable, then that traffic will cease. Increased enforcement and vigorous application of the fullest penalties provided by law are two of the steps in rendering narcotics trade unprofitable. But as long as there is a demand, there will be those willing to take the risks of meeting the demand. So we must also act to destroy the market for drugs, and this means the prevention of new addicts, and the rehabilitation of those who are addicted.

To do this, I am asking the Congress for a total of $105 million in addition to funds already contained in my 1972 budget to be used solely for the treatment and rehabilitation of drug-addicted individuals.

I will also ask the Congress to provide an additional $10 million in funds to increase and improve education and training in the field of dangerous drugs. This will increase the money available for education and training to more than $24 million. It has become fashionable to suppose that no drugs are as dangerous as they are commonly thought to be, and that the use of some drugs entails no risk at all. These are misconceptions, and every day we reap the tragic results of these misconceptions when young people are "turned on" to drugs believing that narcotics addiction is something that happens to other people. We need an expanded effort to show that addiction is all too often a one-way street beginning with "innocent" experimentation and ending in death. Between these extremes is the degradation that addiction inflicts on those who believed that it could not happen to them. . . .

Additional Enforcement Needs

The Comprehensive Drug Abuse Prevention and Control Act of 1970 provides a sound base for the attack on the problem of the availability of narcotics in America. In addition to tighter and more enforceable regulatory controls, the measure provides law enforcement with stronger and better tools. Equally important, the Act contains credible and proper penalties against violators of the drug law. Severe punishments are invoked against the drug pushers and peddlers while more lenient and flexible sanctions are provided for the users. A seller can receive fifteen years for a first offense involving hard narcotics, thirty years if the sale is to a minor, and up to life in prison if the transaction is part of a continuing criminal enterprise.

These new penalties allow judges more discretion, which we feel will restore credibility to the drug control laws and eliminate some of the difficulties prosecutors and judges have had in the past arising out of minimum mandatory penalties for all violators. . . .

Although I do not presently anticipate a necessity for alteration of the purposes or principles of existing enforcement statutes, there is a clear need for some additional enforcement legislation.

To help expedite the prosecution of narcotic trafficking cases, we are asking the Congress to provide legislation which would permit the United States Government to utilize information obtained by foreign police, provided that such information was obtained in compliance with the laws of that country.

We are also asking that the Congress provide legislation which would permit a chemist to submit written findings of his analysis in drug cases. This would speed the process of criminal justice.

The problems of addict identification are equalled and surpassed by the problem of drug identification. To expedite work in this area of narcotics enforcement, I am asking the Congress to provide $2 million to be allotted to the research and development of equipment and techniques for the detection of illegal drugs and drug traffic.

I am asking the Congress to provide $2 million to the Department of Agriculture for research and development of herbicides which can be used to destroy growths of narcotics-producing plants without adverse ecological effects.

International Enforcement

I am asking the Congress to authorize and fund 325 additional positions within the Bureau of Narcotics and Dangerous Drugs to increase their capacity for apprehending those engaged in narcotics trafficking here and abroad and to investigate domestic industrial producers of drugs.

Finally, I am asking the Congress to provide a supplemental appropriation of $25.6 million for the Treasury Department. This will increase funds available to this Department for drug abuse control to nearly $45 million. Of this sum, $18.1 million would be used to enable the Bureau of Customs to develop the technical capacity to deal with smuggling by air and sea, to increase the investigative staff charged with pursuit and apprehension of smugglers, and to increase inspection personnel who search persons, baggage, and cargo entering the country. The remaining $7.5 million would permit the Internal Revenue Service to intensify investigation of persons involved in large-scale narcotics trafficking.

These steps would strengthen our efforts to root out the cancerous growth of narcotics addiction in America. It is impossible to say that the enforcement legislation I have asked for here will be conclusive—that we will not need further legislation. We cannot fully know at this time what further steps will be necessary. As those steps define themselves, we will be prepared to seek further legislation to take any action and every action necessary to wipe out the menace of drug addiction in America. But domestic enforcement alone cannot do the job. If we are to stop the flow of narcotics into the lifeblood of this country, I believe we must stop it at the source.

Gun Control Does Not Deter Crime

David B. Kopel

In the early 1990s a gun control act known as the Brady Bill was put before Congress. Named after White House Press Secretary James Brady, who was shot and disabled during the attempted assassination of President Ronald Reagan in 1981, the bill would require customers to wait seven days for a police background check to occur before being allowed to purchase a gun. In the following statement before the U.S. Senate Subcommittee on the Constitution of the Committee on the Judiciary, David Kopel, attorney, Research Director of the Independence Institute and Associate Policy Analyst at the Cato Institute, argues that the bill would not reduce crime. Kopel emphasizes the fundamental flaw in all gun control legislation, which is that drug dealers and other hardened criminals will always have access to black market guns, regardless of society's attempt to regulate their purchase. Furthermore, Kopel argues that the waiting period will jeopardize law abiding citizens, infringe on their constitutional rights, and prove to be an unnecessary drain on police resources. Despite objections such as these, an amended form of the Brady Bill was signed into law in November 1993.

Citizens should not have to wait for police permission to exercise their Constitutional rights. Reporters who wish to file stories, even about national security matters, should not be required to pre-clear them with government officials. Women who choose to exercise their right to abortion should

David B. Kopel, "Statement of David B. Kopel on S. 466 & H.R. 975 'The Brady Amendment' and S. 1523 Legislation to Amend the Racketeer Influenced Corrupt Organizations Act—Firearms Offenses Proposed as RICO Predicates," before the U.S. Senate Subcommittee on the Constitution of the Committee on the Judiciary, August 2, 1988, www.nysrpa.org/davidkopel.pdf.

not have to submit to a waiting period. Citizens who wish to protect themselves should not have to wait to receive police permission.

Some people wonder why anyone would object to a seven day waiting period [for the purchase of a gun, as required under the proposed Brady Bill]. Seven days is too long for a woman whose ex-boyfriend is threatening to come over and batter her. Seven days is too long for families when a burglar strikes three homes in a neighborhood in one week, and may strike that night. Moreover, the imposition of a waiting period changes the Constitutional right to bear arms into a mere police-granted privilege.

A National Waiting Period Would Not Reduce Gun Crime

Every single study of waiting periods has found them to be absolutely useless in stopping gun crime. [Florida State University] professor Matthew DeZee states "I firmly believe that more restrictive legislation is necessary to reduce the volume of gun crime." Yet his study of waiting period laws showed them to have not the slightest effect. Professors Joseph P. Magaddino and Marshall H. Medoff, both of California State University, Long Beach, came to exactly the same conclusion. Another anti-gun scholar, Duke University's Philip Cook explains: "ineligible people are less likely to submit to the screening process than are eligible people . . . because these people find ways of circumventing the screening system entirely." Cook concludes: "[T]here has been no convincing proof that a police check on handgun buyers reduces violent crime rates." When the Senate Judiciary Committee investigated the issue, the Committee found no evidence that waiting periods affect crime.

Waiting periods have existed in some states for over half a century. Yet after all this time, there is not a single criminological study ever published which shows waiting periods to have any beneficial impact.

The unanimous studies by the criminologists comport with common sense. Said Willis Ross, a former police chief, and currently lobbyist for the Florida Police Chiefs Association: "I think any working policeman will tell you that the crooks already have guns. If a criminal fills out an application and sends his application . . . he's the biggest, dumbest crook I've ever seen."

As a National Institute of Justice study concluded, felons get guns on the street, or from friends, or they steal them. They do not walk into stores, and fill out background check forms.

The Attempted Assasination of Ronald Reagan

Mrs. Sarah Brady, the nation's most prominent anti-gun lobbyist, claims that if the waiting period had been in effect, John Hinckley would not have shot her husband and President [Ronald] Reagan [on March 30, 1981]. As part of the national media campaign in favor of the waiting period, she asserts that Hinckley "lied on his purchase application. Given time, the police could have caught the lie and put him in jail."

That Mrs. Brady . . . use[s] such a demonstrably false anecdote shows how weak [the] case really is. When asked for identification by the gun dealer, Hinckley offered his valid Texas driver's license. The address on the license was Hinckley's last valid address, a rooming house in Lubbock. (At the time of the gun purchase, he had no permanent address.) For the police to find the so-called "lie" would have required them to send an officer to check Hinckley's listed address, and determine that he no longer lived there. Since many police departments do not have the time to visit the scene of residential burglaries, it is rather absurd to expect them to have the time to visit the home of every single prospective handgun buyer.

Moreover, under the Brady amendment, the police would not be verifying Hinckley's address as reported on the federal multiple handgun purchase form. They would only be conducting a background check, and would have found that Hinckley has no criminal or publicly available record or mental illness.

Drug Dealers and Guns

Another inaccuracy in the campaign for a national waiting period is the claim that it will help disarm drug dealers. It is simply preposterous to imagine that any kind of gun legislation, including a waiting period, would have the slightest impact on drug dealers.

Drug dealers obviously cannot count on the police or the courts for protection from violence. Because of this, and because they are a valuable robbery target, it would virtually be suicide for them not to carry a gun.

In addition, drug dealers cannot use normal legal and social commercial dispute resolution mechanisms. Like the gangsters of alcohol prohibition days, drug dealers need guns to protect their business's income and territory. Thus, many drug dealers must own a gun for their lives and their livelihood.

No matter how scarce guns become for civilians, there will always be one for a criminal who can pay enough. Street handguns now sell for less than $100. If the price went up to $2,000, dealers would still buy them, because dealers would have to. Spending a few hours' or days' profits on self-protection is the only logical decision for a dealer. Can anyone really believe that an individual who buys pure heroin by the ounce, who transacts in the highly illegal chemicals used to produce amphetamine, or who sells cocaine on the toughest street-corners in the worst neighborhoods will not know where to buy an illegal gun?

Police Testimony

Several high-ranking police officials, purporting to represent the nation's police, have stated that a waiting period would be beneficial. That testimony is highly dubious.

First of all, it is simply untrue that these police bureaucrats represent the sentiment of the nations's police. In 1987, the Florida Legislature repealed a host of local waiting periods, and that repeal took place thanks to the lobbying of the Florida Police Chiefs Association. In a national survey of all the nation's chiefs of police and sheriffs, 59% percent said that a national 7 day waiting period would not be helpful.

More fundamentally, the opinion of police chiefs is not the arbiter of our Constitutional rights. Some police executives criticize the exclusionary rule; they claim that a strong fourth amendment causes crime. Some police executives criticize the grand jury system, and claim that a strong fifth amendment causes crime. Some criticize the Miranda decision, and claim that a strong sixth amendment causes crime. The police executives here today say that a strong second amendment causes crime. In every case the executives are wrong.

In fact, the actual effect of this legislation will be to decrease crime-fighting resources, and thereby increase crime. There are at least six million handgun transfers per year. How many hours would it take for a policeman to run a national criminal records check, and to visit the home of every person who applied?

One hour, at the very least. That would be six million police hours spent checking up on honest citizens, instead of looking for criminals. In the haystack of applications by honest citizens, police will search for a few needles left by the nation's very stupidest criminals. Looking for crime, police officers will be directed into a paperwork enterprise particularly unlikely to lead to criminals. Wouldn't all those millions of police hours be better spent on patrol; on the streets instead of behind a desk?

The asservations of some police officials that waiting periods have helped them stop large numbers of criminal handgun purchases ought to be taken with a grain of salt. The fact that police officials may deny a handgun permit does not prove that the applicant was a criminal—more likely, that official was capriciously denying a citizen his Constitutional rights. Nor does the fact that an applicant was rejected for unpaid parking tickets or other petty offenses prove that the applicant was a gun criminal. How many applicants were turned down solely because they were once falsely arrested, even though they were later acquitted at a trial? Of the applicants who actually were turned down because of felony convictions, how many did the police immediately arrest and imprison? Any such applicant who was not arrested had the opportunity to buy an illegal gun on the street. . . .

America Must Decriminalize Drugs

Ethan A. Nadelmann

Drugs have not always been illegal. When cocaine became com-
mercially available in the 1880s, it was widely popular in the
United States. Heroin, a patented product of Germany's Bayer
Company, was widely recommended by doctors following its in-
vention in 1889. But by 1900 concerns about the safety and ad-
dictive properties of these drugs had had a dramatic effect on
public opinion, and laws against narcotics began to be enacted.
In 1925 heroin was made illegal, but the drive to criminalize
and punish offenders did not reach its apex until 1956 when the
Narcotics Control Act made the sale of heroin to a person under
eighteen punishable by death. The 1960s saw a resurgence in
recreational drug use and a liberalization of drug laws, which
continued throughout the decade until popular opinion became
once again intolerant of drug use. In 1972 President Richard
Nixon announced the "war on drugs," a policy that President
Ronald Reagan augmented in the 1980s with stiffer sentencing,
strict enforcement, and the use of the military to combat produc-
ers and traffickers.

In 1989 Ethan Nadelmann, a professor of politics and public
affairs, published the following article in the respected journal
Science *in which he argues that the costs and consequences of*
prohibition enforcement outweigh the benefits of drug criminal-
ization. He begins by analyzing the limits of prohibition policies
and reports that the ultimate beneficiaries of such policies are, in
fact, the organized and unorganized drug traffickers who benefit
from the creation of illicit and unregulated markets. The victims
of such policies are the tens of millions of people who continue to

Ethan A. Nadelmann, "Drug Prohibition in the United States: Costs, Consequences, and Alternatives," *Science*, vol. 245, no. 4921, Sept. 1, 1989 pp. 939–47. Copyright 1989 by AAAS. Reproduced by permission of the publisher and the author.

use drugs and risk punishment for an activity that does no harm to others. Furthermore, Nadelmann argues that drug criminalization creates distrust between these otherwise law-abiding citizens and law enforcement, encourages an atmosphere of social intolerance, and violates the principles of a free society.

As frustrations with the drug problem and current drug policies rise daily, growing numbers of political leaders, law enforcement officials, drug abuse experts, and common citizens are insisting that a radical alternative to current policies be fairly considered: the controlled legalization (or decriminalization) of drugs. . . .

There is no one legalization option. At one extreme, some libertarians advocate the removal of all criminal sanctions and taxes on the production and sale of all psychoactive substances—with the possible exception of restriction on sales to children. The alternative extremes are more varied. Some would limit legalization to one of the safest (relatively speaking) of all illicit substances: marijuana. Others prefer a "medical" oversight model similar to today's methadone maintenance programs [a treatment for heroin addicts]. The middle ground combines legal availability of some or all illicit drugs with vigorous efforts to restrict consumption by means other than resorting to criminal sanctions. Many supporters of this dual approach simultaneously advocate greater efforts to limit tobacco consumption and the abuse of alcohol as well as a transfer of government resources from anti-drug law enforcement to drug prevention and treatment. Indeed, the best model for this view of drug legalization is precisely the tobacco control model advocated by those who want to do everything possible to discourage tobacco consumption short of criminalizing the production, sale and use of tobacco.

Clearly, neither drug legalization nor enforcement of anti-drug laws promises to "solve" the drug problem. Nor is there any question that legalization presents certain risks. Legalization would almost certainly increase the availability of drugs, decrease their price, and remove the deterrent power of the criminal sanction—all of which invite increases in drug use and abuse. There are at least three reasons, however, why these risks are worth taking. First, drug control strategies that rely primarily on criminal justice measures are significantly and inherently limited in their capacity to curtail drug abuse. Second, many law enforcement efforts are not only of limited value but also highly costly and counterproductive; indeed, many of the drug-related evils that most people identify as part and parcel of "the drug problem" are in fact the costs of drug prohibition policies. Third, the risks of legalization may well be less than most people assume, particularly if intelligent alternative measures are implemented.

The Limits of Drug Prohibition Policies

Few law enforcement officials any longer contend that their efforts can do much more than they are already doing to reduce drug abuse in the United States. This is true of international drug enforcement efforts, interdiction, and both high-level and street-level domestic drug enforcement efforts.

The United States seeks to limit the export of illicit drugs to this country by a combination of crop eradication and crop substitution programs, financial inducements to growers to abstain from the illicit business, and punitive measures against producers, traffickers, and others involved in the drug traffic. These efforts have met with scant success in the past and show few indications of succeeding in the future. The obstacles are many: marijuana and opium can be grown in a wide variety of locales and even the coca plant "can be grown in virtually any subtropical region of the world which gets between 40 and 240 inches of rain per year, where it never freezes, and where the land is not so swampy as to be waterlogged. In South America, this comes to [approximately] 2,500,000 square miles," of which less than 700 square miles are currently being used to cultivate coca [according to former

Senator Daniel Patrick Moynihan]. Producers in many countries have reacted to crop eradication programs by engaging in "guerilla" farming methods, cultivating their crops in relatively inaccessible hinterlands, and camouflaging them with legitimate crops. Some illicit drug-producing regions are controlled not by the central government but by drug trafficking gangs or political insurgents, thereby rendering eradication efforts even more difficult and hazardous.

Even where eradication efforts prove relatively successful in an individual country, other countries will emerge as new producers, as has occurred with both the international marijuana and heroin markets during the past two decades and can be expected to follow from planned coca eradication programs. The foreign export price of illicit drugs is such a tiny fraction of the retail price in the United States [approximately 4% with cocaine, 1% with marijuana, and much less than 1% with heroin] that international drug control efforts are not even successful in raising the cost of illicit drugs to U.S. consumers. . . .

Law Enforcement Has Little Effect

Domestic law enforcement efforts have proven increasingly successful in apprehending and imprisoning rapidly growing numbers of illicit drug merchants, ranging from the most sophisticated international traffickers to the most common street-level drug dealers. The principal benefit of law enforcement efforts directed at major drug trafficking organizations is probably the rapidly rising value of drug trafficker assets forfeited to the government. There is, however, little indication that such efforts have any significant impact on the price or availability of illicit drugs. Intensive and highly costly street-level law enforcement efforts such as those mounted by many urban police departments in recent years have resulted in the arrests of thousands of low-level drug dealers and users and helped improve the quality of life in targeted neighborhoods.

In most urban centers, however, these efforts have had little impact on the overall availability of illicit drugs.

The logical conclusion of the foregoing analysis is not that criminal justice efforts to stop drug trafficking do not work at all; rather, it is that even substantial fluctuations in those efforts have little effect on the price, availability, and consumption of illicit drugs. The mere existence of criminal laws combined with minimal levels of enforcement is sufficient to deter many potential users and to reduce the availability and increase the price of drugs. Law enforcement officials acknowledge that they alone cannot solve the drug problem but contend that their role is nontheless essential to the overall effort to reduce illicit drug use and abuse. What they are less ready to acknowledge, however, is that the very criminalization of the drug market has proven highly costly and counterproductive in much the same way that the national prohibition of alcohol did 60 years ago. . . .

The Beneficiaries and Victims of Drug Prohibition

The greatest beneficiaries of the drug laws are organized and unorganized drug traffickers. The criminalization of the drug market effectively imposes a de facto value-added tax that is enforced and occasionally augmented by the law enforcement establishment and collected by the drug traffickers. More than half of all organized crime revenues are believed to derive from the illicit drug business; estimates of the dollar value range between $10 and $50 billion per year. By contrast, annual revenues from cigarette bootlegging, which persists principally because of differences among states in their cigarette tax rates, are estimated at between $200 million and $400 million. If the marijuana, cocaine, and heroin markets were legal, state and federal governments would collect billions of dollars annually in tax revenues. Instead, they expend billions in what amounts to a subsidy of organized criminals. . . .

Perhaps the most unfortunate victims of the drug prohibition policies have been the poor and law-abiding residents of urban ghettos. Those policies have proven largely futile in deterring large numbers of ghetto dwellers from becoming drug abusers but they do account for much of what ghetto residents identify as the drug problem. In many neighborhoods, it often seems to be the aggressive gun-toting drug dealers who upset law-abiding residents far more than the addicts nodding out in doorways. Other residents, however, perceive the drug dealers as heroes and successful role models. In impoverished neighborhoods from Medellín and Rio de Janeiro to many leading U.S. cities, they often stand out as symbols of success to children who see no other options. At the same time, the increasingly harsh criminal penalties imposed on adult drug dealers have led to the widespread recruiting of juveniles by drug traffickers. Where once children started dealing drugs only after they had been using them for a few years, today the sequence is often reversed. Many children start to use illegal drugs now only after they have worked for older drug dealers for a while. And the juvenile justice system offers no realistic options for dealing with this growing problem.

Costs and Consequences

Perhaps the most difficult costs to evaluate are those that relate to the widespread defiance of the drug prohibition laws; the effects of labeling as criminals the tens of millions of people who use drugs illicitly, subjecting them to the same risks of criminal sanction, and obliging many of those same people to enter into relationships with drug dealers (who may be criminals in many more senses of the word) in order to purchase their drugs; the cynicism that such laws generate toward other laws and the law in general; and the sense of hostility and suspicion that many otherwise law-abiding individuals feel toward law enforcement officials. It was costs such as these that strongly influenced many of Prohibition's more conservative opponents.

Among the most dangerous consequences of the drug laws are the harms that stem from the unregulated nature of illicit drug production and sale. Many marijuana smokers are worse off for having smoked cannabis that was grown with dangerous fertilizers, sprayed with the herbicide paraquat, or mixed with more dangerous substances. Consumers of heroin and the various synthetic substances sold on the street face even more severe consequences, including fatal overdoses and poisonings from unexpectedly potent or impure drug supplies. In short, nothing resembling an underground Food and Drug Administration has arisen to impose quality control on the illegal drug market and provide users with accurate information on the drugs they consume. More often than not, the quality of a drug addict's life depends greatly on his or her access to reliable supplies. Drug enforcement operations that succeed in temporarily disrupting supply networks are thus a double-edged sword: they encourage some addicts to seek admission into drug treatment programs, but they oblige others to seek out new and hence less reliable suppliers, with the result that more, not fewer, drug-related emergencies and deaths occur. . . .

The Morals of Drug Prohibition

Among the strongest arguments in favor of legalization are the moral ones. On the one hand, the standard refrain regarding the immorality of drug use crumbles in the face of most Americans' tolerance for alcohol and tobacco use. Only the Mormons and a few other like-minded sects, who regard as immoral any intake of substances to alter one's state of consciousness or otherwise cause pleasure, are consistent in this respect; they eschew not just the illicit drugs but also alcohol, tobacco, caffeinated coffee and tea, and even chocolate. "Moral" condemnation by the majority of Americans of some substances and not others is little more than a transient prejudice in favor of some drugs and against others.

On the other hand, drug enforcement involves its own immoralities. Because drug law violations do not create victims with an interest in notifying the police, drug enforcement agents must rely heavily on undercover operations, electronic surveillance, and information provided by informants. In 1986, almost half of the 754 court-authorized orders for wiretaps in the United States involved drug trafficking investigations. These techniques are certainly indispensable to effective law enforcement, but they are also among the least desirable of the tools available to police. The same is true of drug testing. It may be useful and even necessary for determining liability in accidents, but it also threatens and undermines the right of privacy to which many Americans believe they are morally and constitutionally entitled. There are good reasons for requiring that such measures be used sparingly.

Equally disturbing are the increasingly vocal calls for people to inform not just on drug dealers but on neighbors, friends, and even family members who use illicit drugs. Intolerance of illicit drug use and users is heralded not merely as an indispensable ingredient in the war against drugs but as a mark of good citizenship. Certainly every society requires citizens to assist in the enforcement of criminal laws. But societies, particularly democratic and pluralistic ones, also rely strongly on an ethic of tolerance toward those who are different but do no harm to others. Overzealous enforcement of the drug laws risks undermining that ethic and propagating in its place a society of informants. Indeed, enforcement of drug laws makes a mockery of an essential principle of a free society, that those who do no harm to others should not be harmed by others, and particularly not by the state. Most of the nearly 40 million Americans who illegally consume drugs each year do no direct harm to anyone else; indeed, most do relatively little harm even to themselves. Directing criminal and other sanctions at them, and rationalizing the justice of such sanctions, may well represent the greatest societal cost of our current drug prohibition system.

Three Strikes Laws Reduce Crime

Dan Lungren

Although three strikes laws have been enacted in more than half of U.S. states, California's controversial 1994 version stands out as the most comprehensive and punitive. Generally speaking, three strikes laws require a judge to sentence a criminal found guilty of three or more felony offences to a minimum of twenty-five years to life in prison. California's statute is unique for two reasons. First, it doubles sentences for a second strike. Second, the crime that triggers the life sentence can be any *felony, including such arguably less serious offences as theft or the possession of small amounts of drugs.*

Critics have pointed out that sixty-five percent of those imprisoned under this law in California were convicted of non-violet crimes and 354 of them received twenty-five-years-to-life sentences for petty theft of less than $250. They argue that the law is unnecessarily harsh, unfairly locking people away who pose a minimal threat to society. Proponents argue that such cases are justifiable as they are the result of a law that makes the state safer for law-abiding citizens. In the following article published two years after the instigation of the three strikes law, attorney general of California Dan Lungren, who held this position from 1991 to 1996, reports that it has had a positive, immediate, and quantifiable effect on California's crime rate. Lungren argues that this drop in the crime rate is due to the deterrent effect of tough laws, the imprisonment of habitual recitivists and the migration of paroled felons leaving California.

Crime in California is dropping—fast. So far, this decade looks to be the most promising for reducing crime since the state started keeping complete statistics in 1952. Although

Dan Lungren, "Three Cheers for Three Strikes: California Enjoys a Record Drop in Crime," *Policy Review*, no. 80, November–December 1996. Reproduced by permission.

California suffered—along with the rest of the nation—while the crime rate nearly quadrupled between 1960 and 1980, California is now recording some of the largest crime reductions of any state. . . .

What accounts for these astonishing numbers? I would suggest it is in large part due to California's passage of a "three strikes and you're out" law, which has done more to stop revolving-door justice than any other measure in state or federal law. Enacted in 1994 by both popular initiative and legislative action, the law requires a defendant convicted of a felony to serve an indeterminate life sentence when it is proved that he has committed two or more previous felonies defined as "violent" or "serious." Offenders given a life sentence become eligible for parole only after serving twenty-five years or three times the term that the current conviction would ordinarily warrant, whichever is greater. A "two strikes" provision, part of the same law, requires that when a defendant is convicted of a felony, and has been previously convicted of one "serious or violent" felony, the term of imprisonment is twice the usual sentence provided for the second felony conviction. . . .

Accountability for Criminal Choices

As written and applied, "three strikes" is a model of strict and even-handed justice. It demands accountability, reflects common sense, presents a clear and certain penalty, and uncompromisingly invests in public safety. I like to reflect on former Chief Justice Warren Burger's comments made before an American Bar Association meeting in 1981: "A far greater factor is the deterrent effect of swift and certain consequences: swift arrest, prompt trial, certain penalty and—at some point—finality of judgment." Can anybody believe otherwise? The quotation reflects the chief justice's fundamental understanding that the rule of law affords the complementary blessings of both freedom and responsibility and provides the governing framework in which individual citizens make their individual decisions. The rule of law protects our free will from arbitrary constraints; at the same time, it provides consistency and impartiality to the life of the state and its citizens. What seems obvious in this formula is that as individuals exercise their individual, personal liberties in living their lives and in interacting with others, they also become personally accountable for the choices they make—choices from which clear consequences arise.

Yet, many opponents of "three strikes" disagree with the notion of strict personal accountability. Of course, while most of the self-proclaimed experts in criminal justice state their objections on other grounds—they call "three strikes" draconian, ineffective, too broad, too tough, and too expensive—the real theme that resounds in their criticism is that "three strikes" "re-victimizes" persons who already have been "victimized" by the forces of an unfriendly society and an adversarial government. In short, their view is that the targets of "three strikes" are not accountable for their conduct because "complex" forces extrinsic to the individual are the principal causes of criminal activity: poor education, unemployment, a detrimental social situation, or even the law enforcement system. Further, these critics have employed this philosophy to demand that sentencing for convicted criminals be made in light of "mitigating circumstances" and that incarceration should be for "rehabilitative purposes" to redress what society "did" to the inmate.

The voters of California have rejected this nonsense. And the record shows "three strikes" is doing precisely what the voters demanded when they overwhelmingly passed the initiative, by 72 percent to 28. The career criminal with multiple serious or violent felony convictions is being forced to make what should be an easy decision: Either stop committing felonies and live the remainder of your life in freedom, or spend 25 years to life in prison the next time you are caught and convicted of a felony. The career criminal will be held *personally accountable* for his decisions. Imagine that! When the voters rejected revolving-door justice, they rejected the arguments of apologists that we can divorce negative personal conduct from individual accountability.

Proportional Punishment

The second criticism against "three strikes" by criminal apologists is that the law does not furnish proportionate punishment. These critics focus on the cases in which a habitual felon is charged with a "minor" property or drug offense that qualifies as a third strike. They allege it is wholly improper to impose an indeterminate life sentence for a "minor" crime and that instead the offender should be given special consideration or more lenient treatment. The philosophical approach advocated here is that criminal conduct should be viewed in isolation of past history and surrounding circumstances. If a habitual felon currently commits a crime that is classified as a felony under California law, and he has convictions for two previous "serious" felonies, is it any surprise that Californians want a tougher punishment for the current felony?

Let's examine what constitutes a "serious or violent felony" for a "three strikes" prior conviction: murder or voluntary manslaughter; mayhem; rape; sodomy by force, violence, duress, menace, threat of great bodily injury, or fear of immediate and unlawful bodily injury on the victim or another person; oral copulation by force, violence, duress, et cetera; lewd or lascivious acts on children; felonies with personal use of firearm; attempted murder; assault with intent to commit rape or robbery; assault with deadly weapon; arson; kidnapping; selling drugs to minors; and many others. If these are not "serious" enough, I would like to know which ones should be dropped as insufficiently serious. When the third strike is but a "minor" felony, such as grand theft or possession of certain drugs for sale, why should society ignore the habitual criminal activity of this offender when sentencing him?

Common sense dictates the answer to this question. First, society does not view crime in a vacuum. As Princeton professor John Dilulio recently wrote, "Most Americans rightly think in terms of total criminality—the full social and moral weight of an offender's acts against life, liberty, and property. They reject the criminological equivalent of grade inflation—judging plea-bargained-gorged prisoners by their last conviction rather than their overall criminal grade-point average, adult and juvenile." Second, an offender who has committed a series of violent or serious crimes is likely to commit additional crimes of the same nature; wisdom demands that an offender's criminal record be the starting point for determining punishment. Finally, the rule of law demands a response to a lifestyle of destruction and violence. There is nothing disproportionate about giving a harsh sentence to a felon who has not learned from having committed two serious felonies before.

Deterrence Effect

There has been a marked split of opinion, at least in academia, as to how best to prevent crime. On the one hand, some argue that habitual criminal activity can be "cured" by placing offenders in correctional programs that renounce retributive goals and instead stress the redemptive value of education, vocational instruction, and even group therapy. Another school of thought centers on the positive behavioral effects of a system of clear and certain consequences for destructive and criminal behavior. Unfortunately, many in the "redemptive programs" group reject outright the legitimacy of deterrence. The causes of criminal behavior are far too complex, they say, to permit any generalizations about whether individuals will consider legal prohibitions or sanctions when they act and interact in society—especially when they are hungry, ill-housed, under-educated, or emotionally neglected.

The value of deterrence, however, is grossly underestimated by these "experts," who have devised no way to prove or disprove its effects. I believe certainty of incarceration, for a long and inevitable period, nonetheless has a dramatic effect on the behavior of individuals. Consider the statement of a veteran homicide detective in the Sacramento police department as to the law's impact: "You hear [the criminals] talking about it all the time. These guys are really squirming. They know what's going on. . . . I've flipped 100 percent," Gregory Gaines told a *Sacramento Bee* reporter. Gaines had just been released from Folsom State Prison with two serious or violent felony convictions—two "strikes"—and told the reporter that many other inmates have decided to heed the warnings of the "three strikes" law. "It's a brand-new me, mainly because of the law. It's going to keep me working, keep my attitude adjusted."

Perhaps the most interesting statistics track the migratory patterns of felons on parole in California. In the last year before "three strikes" became law in 1994, 226 more paroled felons chose to move to California than moved out. After "three strikes" took effect, the flow reversed: 1,335 more paroled felons chose to leave California in 1995 than to enter. We've gone from being a net importer of paroled felons to a net exporter! Coincidence? Hardly.

Gun Control Prevents Crime

William J. Clinton

On April 20, 1999, two students at Columbine High School in Littleton, Colorado, shot and killed twelve students and a teacher before turning their weapons on themselves. The massacre immediately reignited the gun-control debate. In the following speech delivered in December 1999, President William J. Clinton argues that strong gun control legislation will reduce violent crime. Clinton had already passed two controversial gun control laws, the 1993 Brady Handgun Violence Prevention Act, which required customers to wait five days so that a background check could be performed by police before purchasing a gun, and a 1994 ban on semiautomatic assault weapons. Clinton argues that these laws must be strengthened in order to close loopholes that allow civilians unrestrained access to these weapons and proposes new legislation that would make adults criminally responsible if they failed to keep firearms away from juveniles. According to Clinton, America's gun culture must be changed out of an obligation to save children's lives.

I want to begin by saying a lot of people have made remarkable contributions, I think, to this effort to get us to look at the violence of our culture and how it makes the most vulnerable of our children, without regard to their income or their social status, closer to the line of taking violent action, and how it complicates family life for everyone. . . .

Cultural Challenges

But if you believe that we have special cultural challenges, it seems to me that that's an argument that we ought to bend over backwards to try to remove the opportunities for bad

William J. Clinton, "Remarks Announcing Proposed Gun Control Legislation, April 27, 1999," *Weekly Compilation of Presidential Documents*, May 3, 1999, www.highbeam.com.

things happening, if we have more kids that are vulnerable to doing those things, not an argument that we ought to say, "Well, we should walk away from that and just try to make sure everybody, individually, in the whole country, never does anything wrong."

And what's the real problem here? The problem is, we have another culture in our country that I think has gotten confused about its objectives. We have a huge hunting and sport shooting culture in America, and unlike many of you, I grew up in it. I was 12 years old the first time I took a .22 and shot it at a can on a fencepost in the country. I know about this.

We always talk about the NRA [National Rifle Association]; the NRA has been powerful not only because they have a lot of money but because they can influence people who vote. And in that culture, people believe everybody should be personally responsible for their actions; if you just punish people who do wrong more harshly, fewer people will do wrong; and everybody tells me I've got a constitutional right to keep and bear arms, so don't fool with me; and every reasonable restriction is just the camel's nose in the tent, and pretty soon they'll come after my shotgun, and I'll miss the next duck hunting season.

And we smile about that, but there are some people who would be on this platform today who lost their seats in 1994 because they voted for the Brady bill, [which mandates a five day waiting period for the purchase of a gun] and they voted for the assault weapons ban, and they did it in areas where people could be frightened. And the voters had not had enough time, which they did have within 2 more years, to see that nobody was going to take their gun away.

Reasonable Laws

So we have more than one cultural problem here. And I want to make a plea to everybody who is waiting for the next deer season in my home state to think about this in terms of what our reasonable obligations to the larger community of America are.

Do we know for absolutely certain that if we had every reasonable law and the ones I'm going to propose here that none of these school violence things would have happened? No. But we do know one thing for certain. We know there would have been fewer of them, and there would have been fewer kids killed in the last several years in America. We know that for certain. We know that.

Cultures are hard to change. And cultures should never be used to avoid individual responsibility. But we—when we get to where we change, then we wonder. We look back and we say, "How could we have ever done it otherwise?"

Let me ask you something. Next time you get on an airplane, think about how you'd feel if the headline in the morning paper right before you got on the airplane was "Airport Metal Detectors and X-Ray Machines Abolished as Infringement on Americans' Constitutional Right To Travel." Think about it. That's the headline in the morning paper. And right next to it there is another headline, "Terrorist Groups Expanding Operations in the United States." And you read the two headlines, and you're getting on the airplane, exercising your constitutional right to travel, which is now no longer infringed by the fact that you might have to go through the metal detector twice and take out your money clip or take off your heavily metaled belt and that somebody is x raying your luggage as it gets on the airplane. It's unthinkable now, isn't it? This will become unthinkable, too, that we should ever reverse these things if we ever have enough sense to do them.

But we still have a cultural and a political argument that says to defend Americans' rights to reasonable hunting and sport shooting, you have to defend the indefensible, as well. This is—it doesn't make any sense at all, unless you're caught up in this sort of web of distorted logic and denial. . . .

The Legitimate Right to Hunt

So it's not just a culture of violence that has to change; it's the culture of hunting and sport shooting that has to stop financing efforts to frighten their members, who are good, God-fearing, law-abiding, taxpaying citizens out there, into believing that every time we try to save a kid's life, it's a camel's nose in the tent.

I have had to go through those metal detectors as many as three times, back when I had a real life and I was traveling around, because I had all kinds of stuff in there and every time I start to get a little aggravated, I think, "Boy, I don't want that plane to blow up." You know, make me go through a dozen times if you want to. And the person behind me.

Now, we've got to think about this in that way. These are the folks we have to reach. When there are no constituents for this movement, the movement will evaporate. When people from rural Pennsylvania and rural West Virginia and rural Colorado and Idaho start calling their Congressmen and saying, "Hey, man, we can live with this. We can live with this. This is no big deal, you know? I mean, we're just out there doing what we do. We'll gladly put up with an extra hassle, a little wait, a little this, a little that, because we want to save several thousand kids a year."

That is my challenge to you. That is what is going on.

Now, here are the things we want to do. A lot of you won't think they're enough, but you remember the culture. You change the culture; we'll change the laws. You change the message; we'll do it. And none of them have anything to do with anybody's legitimate right to hunt.

The Gun Show Loophole

First of all, we ought to strengthen the Brady law. . . . The States now have the insta-check system [to determine if gun purchasers are eligible to own a weapon], which is good. The mandatory waiting period has expired. That's bad because we need it in addition to the insta-check system to give a cooling-off period to people who are in a fit of rage. It's important.

The law that we would present, the act, will also prevent juveniles who commit violent crimes from ever buying a gun. It would apply the Brady law's prohibition to juvenile violence. It would require Brady background checks on anyone who wants to buy explosives. Very important. And it would abolish, at long last, as Senator [Dianne] Feinstein said, a dangerous loophole that was likely exploited in Littleton, which allows people to buy weapons at gun shows without any background checks at all.

Now, you need to go make this case on this gun show deal. I don't know how many of you have ever been to one of these gun shows. I've been to gun shows in rural America. People walk around, and they've got their cars, and they've got their trunk open, and people walk in and say, "This is nice, and that's nice," and "This is a 100-year-old rifle," and blah, blah, blah. And then they say, "This is just too much hassle, you know. . . ."—so, it's going to be a hassle for them. It's worth it. It's worth it. We're sorry. It's worth it.

You don't have to pretend it won't be a hassle. Tell them you know it will be a hassle. It's worth it. People's lives are at stake here. What these shows started out doing, which was a good way for people who live in rural areas—it started out primarily in rural areas—who enjoy hunting and are interested in different kinds of weapons, to have an interesting experience on a weekend afternoon—has turned out to be a gaping loophole through which criminals and deranged people and other people get guns they could not otherwise get.

And so we have to say, "We haven't asked you to abolish your gun shows, but we've asked you to undergo the inconvenience necessary to save more lives." We don't have to be insensitive; we just have to be determined. But I'm telling you, if we don't do something about this gun show loophole, we're going to continue to have serious, serious problems. And it's very important.

Strengthen the Assault Weapons Ban

The second thing we've got to do is to strengthen the assault weapons ban, to close the loophole that allows dealers to sell older, high-capacity ammunition magazines manufactured abroad. Now, I bet . . . , you thought, now, who in the world could be against this? I actually had a conversation with a Member of Congress who said to me . . . , "But you've got to understand, we've got people who use these bigger magazines for certain kinds of sport contests." And I said, "Well, so what?" But he said, "They'll beat me if I vote for this." I said, "They'll beat you if they think all you're doing is making their lives miserable because some Washington bureaucrat asked you to do it. If you can explain to them that it's worth a minor alteration in their sporting habits to save people's lives, they won't beat you."

But my point is, you've got to help these people. . . . They don't like this because they don't understand that if they do what you're asking them to do, they can save a lot of lives. And we have got to fix this. This is just pure mathematics; you're going to have fewer people die if you get rid of these magazines. So you need to go out there where the problem is and debate your fellow citizens and discuss it with them. It's important.

Guns and Juveniles

The third thing the legislation would do is to raise the legal age of handgun possession from 18 to 21 years. It would also strengthen our zero tolerance for guns in schools, which, as one of the previous members said, had led us to 6,000 suspensions or expulsions last year, by requiring schools to report to the police any student who brings a gun to school and requiring that the student get counseling. That, I think, is very important.

The provision holding adults criminally responsible would only apply, but—this is quite important but it would apply if they recklessly failed to keep firearms out of the reach of young people. This would mandate a steep increase in penalties for adults who transfer guns illegally to juveniles. It would require child safety locks to be sold with all new guns.

Finally, it would crack down on illegal gun trafficking, doubling the number of cities now working with the Bureau of Alcohol, Tobacco and Firearms to trace every gun seized by the police. . . .

It would require that dealers submit information not only on the guns they sell but on used guns, which are often very hard for law enforcement agencies to trace. It would significantly increase penalties for gun runners caught trafficking large numbers of firearms. It would establish a national system, as soon as it's feasible, to limit handgun purchases to one a month, following the lead of Virginia. . . .

Saving Children's Lives

One Senator called me the night before last and said he'd had a town meeting in his State with children. And he asked how many of the schoolchildren had actually talked to their parents about what happened in Littleton. And only 10 percent of the kids raised their hands. And one child said, "I had to go and turn off the television and tell my parents we were going to talk about it." She said, "They're just scared. They're scared. They didn't know how to talk about it."

So there are all these cultural issues. And then there's this big cultural issue of the gun and sport hunting culture. And I hope that—a lot of my folks at home might take offense at what I said today, but I'm trying to help explain them to you. And I felt comfortable taking on these issues, and I thought maybe I was in a unique position to take on all these gun issues all these years because of where I grew up and because I understand how people think who don't agree with this.

But I'm telling you, we've got to keep working until people start thinking about this stuff the same way they think about x rays and metal detectors at airports. That's the goal. We have to redefine the national community so that we have a shared obligation to save children's lives. And we've got to get out of this crazy denial that this won't make a difference. It's crazy; it won't make—just because it won't make all the difference doesn't mean it won't make a difference. It will make a difference.

Stiff Prison Sentences Deter Crime

Morgan Reynolds

In the following selection Morgan Reynolds, a professor of labor economics at Texas A&M University and former director of the Criminal Justice Center at the National Center for Policy Analysis, argues that there is a direct correlation between the increasing number of criminals incarcerated in the 1990s and the drop in crime rates during that same period. Reynolds uses the findings of several studies to argue that the single most effective way to reduce crime is to mete out stiff sentences, in opposition to the prevailing notion that one must first tackle the "root causes" of crime. According to Reynolds, prisons have two goals: to punish criminals and deter crime, and nowhere is this more effective than with juvenile offenders. For Reynolds, a "nationwide decline in family, character formation and personal restraint" has led to increased rates of juvenile offending, and the best thing that society can do in order to set young offenders straight is to impose strong "external restraints" in the form of prison sentences.

Prisons have broken the back of our 35-year crime wave. It's about that simple.

An estimated 1.8 million inmates were in prisons and jails at midyear 1998—double the number behind bars a decade earlier. A Justice Department study finds that the average time spent by violent criminals in state prisons rose to 49 months in 1997 from only 43 months in 1993. Prison growth has begun to moderate, however, with last year's 4.4 percent increase below the average 6.2 percent increase in the 1990s.

Lo and behold, as prisons filled, crime fell. The FBI's crime index has declined for seven straight years. Every category of crime is lower than in 1991. The national murder rate is down by more than one-third and down an astounding 70 percent in New York City, the lowest since 1964. Four years ago, almost 22,000 people were murdered, a majority of them African-American. Last year, only 17,000 went to their graves as homicides. Robberies reported to the police have declined by more than 100,000 crimes in only three years. In much of the nation, crime is lower than at any time since the 1960s and almost everyone feels safer.

In 1991 Eugene Methvin, a highly regarded crime analyst, calculated that about 75,000 new, hard-core, violent repeaters were added to our population every year. Locking all of them up from their third-felony conviction until age 30 would boost the prison population to 1.2 million, our total today. Methvin concluded that this would produce "a sharp drop in our horrendous crime rates." While the justice system undoubtedly has been less efficient in its selection of offenders than his calculation demanded, Methvin's prediction nevertheless has been confirmed.

How could locking up almost one million more bad guys for longer terms fail to cut crime? It's difficult to deny this proposition, but count on the experts to try. They would have us believe that if we released nearly a million inmates today, it would have no impact on crime.

Prisons Make Crime Less Attractive

Instead of common sense, the elite express caution, celebrate complexity or push obscure explanations for the drop in crime—anything to avoid the conclusion that getting tough works by changing criminal choices. Alfred Blumstein, a criminologist at Carnegie-Mellon University in Pittsburgh, labels the connection between falling crime and filling prisons "too simplistic." Apparently, only complicated stuff is good. Pointing out the obvious is bad form.

As with educational theory, criminology long has been a field driven by fads. Lacking a solid intellectual anchor and populated primarily by sociologists, criminology for the most part has ignored the impact of law enforcement on crime because it was assumed that the risks of punishment didn't enter into offenders' calculations. In fact, most social scientists avoid the word "choice" or calculation in favor of terms such as "precursor," "correlate," "at risk" and influence. Journalists duly follow.

Sometimes, however, a serious academic strays into the real world of criminal behavior. The late psychologist Richard Herrnstein, for example, wrote that the real cause of crime is "people for whom the positive side of the ledger sufficiently outweighs the negative side and who have the opportunity for breaking the law."

The "negative side" of the ledger is exactly what the criminal-justice system is supposed to do: Mete out appropriately bad consequences for bad choices. For a nation dedicated to individual freedom, individual responsibility and equality before the law, denial of liberty for thugs is fitting punishment. The system actually is taking this job seriously again, and it is working. Crime has become less attractive, and adults (at least) are avoiding entry into the industry or fleeing it.

Even the *New York Times* concedes that "a remarkably optimistic new view of crime prevention is emerging among experts, and their revised consensus suggests that law enforcement may make a critical difference after all."

Public Opinion Endorses Punishment

In 1950, the odds of going to prison for a serious crime of violence or burglary were 5.3 percent, and crime was low. By 1970, the odds had collapsed to 1.3 percent and, by the end of the decade, had recovered to only 1.6 percent. In fact, during the crime explosion of the 1960s and 1970s, the absolute number of new-adult commitments to prisons for serious crimes of violence and burglary actually declined, while the number of such crimes reported to the police nearly tripled. The system became a bad joke. By 1990, however, the odds of prison time had increased to 2.4 percent and, by 1997, to 2.9 percent.

Expected punishment has been boosted at each stage of the criminal-justice process. In some neighborhoods, community-oriented policing has restored trust between citizens and police, leading to more arrests. Aggressive enforcement against minor infractions has allowed police to charge suspects with more serious crimes based on outstanding warrants for arrest.

Additional prosecutors backed by tougher laws have raised conviction rates. New-prison construction has allowed officials to make convicts serve more of their sentences.

Many criminologists oppose punishment on ideological rather than logical or evidential grounds, believing it cruel and outmoded. Supposedly, only rehabilitation is good. Yet, except for the issue of locking up juveniles, the public never bought into this mumbo jumbo. Almost uniformly across groups, public opinion endorses punishment. More than three-quarters of the public believe that punishment is the primary justification for sentencing. More than 70 percent believe that incarceration is the only sure way to prevent future crimes, and more than three-quarters believe that the courts are too easy on criminals. Three-quarters favor the death penalty for first-degree murder.

The public realizes that nice doesn't always work. There always have been thieves, murderers and rapists and always will be. As long as man is a free moral agent who can choose between good and evil, we'll have evil actions. No amount of rehabilitation, early intervention, personality profiling and therapy will change that.

Criminals are Not Punished

Incentives matter in crime just as in other aspects of life. Interviews with criminals provide the strongest evidence that they reason and act much like other human beings. Courts have been handing out tougher punishment, and criminals know it. As more criminals get convicted under new truth-in-sentencing laws, which require convicts to serve 85 percent of their sentences, their sabbatical leaves from society, at taxpayer expense, will lengthen even more.

Seeing that the law means business, many potential criminals decide to stay out of the law's way. As social scientist Charles Murray summed it up recently: "We figured out what to do with criminals. Innovations in policing helped, but the key insight was an old one: Lock 'em up."

Yes, it would be better if young males would straighten up before they become adult criminals. Focus on "prison prevention" rather than prison, as the liberals say. Yet here lies our biggest failure. Studies conclude that punishment works, especially for juveniles, but juvenile systems too often fail to apply the lesson.

Psychologist Sarnoff Mednick of the University of Southern California, for example, compared the records of thousands of young Philadelphia and Danish criminals. He found that 60 percent of those arrested four and five times in Denmark were punished compared with only 14 percent in Philadelphia. "The big problem with our handling of criminals in America is that they're not punished," says Mednick. Many are surprised to hear that, in view of the nation's relatively high number of adult prisons. Yet, often the first time a young man makes his way to jail or prison is his first punishment, . . . [he has had] an active criminal career with dozens of crimes and several arrests.

Punishment for Juveniles Should Be Harsh

During the 1980s and 1990s, adult crime declined while juvenile crime increased. For example, serious violent crimes committed by adults reached a 25-year low in 1997, according to the annual National Crime Victimization Survey, while the number committed by juveniles remained well above their 1986 low. More dramatically, the arrest rate for violent crimes rose three times faster for juveniles than for adults between 1978 and 1993.

Why? One clue is that youths typically reduce their criminal involvement at the age of majority, suggesting a response to incentives. Apparently, youthful lawbreakers take the prospect of adult jail or prison time more seriously than juvenile sanctions.

This view has been confirmed in a recent study by economist Steve Levitt of the University of Chicago. Levitt used state data from 1978 to 1993 and found that most of the rise in juvenile crime has been a response to softer and softer treatment of young criminals. The drop in criminal activity at the age of majority is largest in states where the juvenile system is lenient and the adult system is tough. By contrast, criminal activity goes up at the age of majority in states with harsh juvenile courts and lenient adult courts.

States more likely to put youths into secure custody enjoy lower rates of juvenile offending, and the deterrent effect is stronger than that for adults. What seems to matter both to adults and to youth is the current law-enforcement sanctions facing each group, not contemporary sanctions for the other group.

So are jails and prisons panaceas? Of course not. The infamous "root causes"—poverty, failed public schools and out-of-wedlock births—matter, too. Thirty years ago, one in three African-American babies was born out of wedlock. Today it's seven out of ten, and white illegitimacy rates have jumped to one in four. Billions of federal dollars have—with the best of intentions—subsidized irresponsibility and ruined millions of lives. But the nationwide decline in family, character formation and personal restraint means that external restraints are all the more important.

Many reforms could alleviate our dependence on incarceration, including more responsible parenting, competitive inner-city schools, private restitution for victims and a retreat in the federal government's disastrous war on drugs. But that's another story. The hard reality is that there must be consequences for criminal behavior, and that means prison space.

The Patriot Act Deters Crime

John Ashcroft

In the aftermath of the terrorist attacks of September 11, 2001, many argued that law enforcement required additional powers in order to preserve the safety of American citizens and that these additional powers would require a renegotiation of some civil liberties such as the citizen's rights to privacy. Introduced in the House of Representatives on October 23, 2001, Congress passed the USA PATRIOT Act [Uniting and Strengthening America by Providing Appropriate Tools Required to Intercept and Obstruct Terrorism] with remarkable speed and almost no debate. It was signed into law by President George W. Bush just three days later. The main goal of the act was to expand the authority of law enforcement to detect and battle terrorism, though it was also intended to enable the prosecution of other crimes. Critics argued that the act violates some fundamental rights guaranteed by the Constitution by giving the government access to citizen's medical, financial, phone and Internet records, information about the books one buys or borrows, and the right to conduct secret searches of homes. Proponents argued that the act would make immigration more secure, money laundering more easy to detect, and penalties for would-be terrorists more severe.

In the following testimony before the Senate Committee on the Judiciary on December 6, 2001, Attorney General John Ashcroft, who held the position from 2001 to 2005, defends the legitimacy and necessity of the act. Ashcroft argues that because terrorists exploit the openness of a free society, law enforcement requires increased surveillance capabilities in order to identify the terrorist threat that operates within. Furthermore, he argues that these additional tools do not compromise civil liberties in any meaningful way and will be used responsibly in the defence of the nation.

John Ashcroft, "Testimony of Attorney General John Ashcroft, Senate Committee on the Judiciary, December 6, 2001," www.usdoj.gov.

On the morning of September 11, as the United States came under attack, I was in an airplane with several members of the Justice Department en route to Milwaukee, in the skies over the Great Lakes. By the time we could return to Washington, thousands of people had been murdered at the World Trade Center. One hundred eighty-nine were dead at the Pentagon. Forty-four had crashed to the ground in Pennsylvania. From that moment, at the command of the President of the United States, I began to mobilize the resources of the Department of Justice toward one single, over-arching and over-riding objective: to save innocent lives from further acts of terrorism.

America's campaign to save innocent lives from terrorists is now [in December 2001] eighty-seven days old. It has brought me back to this committee to report to you in accordance with Congress's oversight role. I welcome this opportunity to clarify for you and the American people how the Justice Department is working to protect American lives while preserving American liberties. . . .

The Crime of Terrorism

Under the leadership of President Bush, America has made the choice to fight terrorism—not just for ourselves but for all civilized people. Since September 11, through dozens of warnings to law enforcement, a deliberate campaign of terrorist disruption, tighter security around potential targets, and a preventative campaign of arrest and detention of lawbreakers, America has grown stronger—and safer—in the face of terrorism.

Thanks to the vigilance of law enforcement and the patience of the American people, we have not suffered another major terrorist attack. Still, we cannot—we must not—allow ourselves to grow complacent. The reasons are apparent to me each morning. My day begins with a review of the threats to Americans and American interests that were received in the previous twenty-four hours. If ever there were proof of the existence of evil in the world, it is in the pages of these reports. They are a chilling daily chronicle of hatred of America by fanatics who seek to extinguish freedom, enslave women, corrupt education and to kill Americans wherever and whenever they can.

The terrorist enemy that threatens civilization today is unlike any we have ever known. It slaughters thousands of innocents—a crime of war and a crime against humanity. It seeks weapons of mass destruction and threatens their use against America. No one should doubt the intent, nor the depth, of its consuming, destructive hatred.

Terrorist operatives infiltrate our communities—plotting, planning and waiting to kill again. They enjoy the benefits of our free society even as they commit themselves to our destruction. They exploit our openness—not randomly or haphazardly—but by deliberate, premeditated design. . . .

Strengthening Laws

Mr. Chairman and members of the committee, we are at war with an enemy who abuses individual rights as it abuses jet airliners: as weapons with which to kill Americans. We have responded by redefining the mission of the Department of Justice. Defending our nation and its citizens against terrorist attacks is now our first and overriding priority.

We have launched the largest, most comprehensive criminal investigation in world history to identify the killers of September 11 and to prevent further terrorist attacks. Four thousand FBI agents are engaged with their international counterparts in an unprecedented worldwide effort to detect, disrupt and dismantle terrorist organizations.

We have created a national task force at the FBI to centralize control and information sharing in our investigation. This task force has investigated hundreds of thousands of leads, conducted over 500 searches, interviewed thousands of witnesses and obtained numerous court-authorized surveillance orders. Our prosecutors and agents have collected information and evidence from countries throughout Europe and the Middle East.

Immediately following the September 11 attacks, the Bureau of Prisons acted swiftly to intensify security precautions in connection with all al Qaeda [the terrorist organization that carried out the September 11 attacks] and other terrorist inmates, increasing perimeter security at a number of key facilities.

We have sought and received additional tools from Congress. Already, we have begun to utilize many of these tools. Within hours of passage of the USA PATRIOT Act, we made use of its provisions to begin enhanced information sharing between the law-enforcement and intelligence communities. We have used the provisions allowing nationwide search warrants for e-mail and subpoenas for payment information. And we have used the act to place those who access the Internet through cable companies on the same footing as everyone else.

Enforcing Laws

Just yesterday, at my request, the State Department designated thirty-nine entities as terrorist organizations pursuant to the USA PATRIOT Act.

We have waged a deliberate campaign of arrest and detention to remove suspected terrorists who violate the law from our streets. Currently, we have brought criminal charges against 110 individuals, of whom 60 are in federal custody. The INS [Immigration and Naturalization Services] has detained 563 individuals on immigration violations.

We have investigated more than 250 incidents of retaliatory violence and threats against Arab Americans, Muslim Americans, Sikh Americans and South Asian Americans.

Since September 11, the Customs Service and Border Patrol have been at their highest state of alert. All vehicles and persons entering the country are subjected to the highest level of scrutiny. Working with the State Department, we have imposed new screening requirements on certain applicants for non-immigrant visas. At the direction of the President, we have created a Foreign Terrorist Tracking Task Force to ensure that we do everything we can to prevent terrorists from entering the country, and to locate and remove those who already have.

We have prosecuted to the fullest extent of the law individuals who waste precious law enforcement resources through anthrax hoaxes [which cropped up after the September 11 attacks].

We have offered non-citizens willing to come forward with valuable information a chance to live in this country and one day become citizens.

We have forged new cooperative agreements with Canada to protect our common borders and the economic prosperity they sustain. . . .

Balancing Rights and Security

In all these ways and more, the Department of Justice has sought to prevent terrorism with reason, careful balance and excruciating attention to detail. Some of our critics, I regret to say, have shown less affection for detail. Their bold declarations of so-called fact have quickly dissolved, upon inspection, into vague conjecture. Charges of "kangaroo courts" and "shredding the Constitution" give new meaning to the term, "the fog of war."

Since lives and liberties depend upon clarity, not obfuscation, and reason, not hyperbole, let me take this opportunity today to be clear: Each action taken by the Department of Justice, as well as the war crimes commissions considered by the President and the Department of Defense, is carefully drawn to target a narrow class of individuals—terrorists. Our legal powers are targeted at terrorists. Our investigation is focused on terrorists. Our prevention strategy targets the terrorist threat. . . .

Our efforts have been carefully crafted to avoid infringing on constitutional rights while saving American lives. We have engaged in a deliberate campaign of arrest and detention of law breakers. All persons being detained have the right to contact their lawyers and their families. Out of respect for their privacy, and concern for saving lives, we will not publicize the names of those detained.

We have the authority to monitor the conversations of 16 of the 158,000 federal inmates and their attorneys because we suspect that these communications are facilitating acts of terrorism. Each prisoner has been told in advance his conversations will be monitored. None of the information that is protected by attorney-client privilege may be used for prosecution. Information will only be used to stop impending terrorist acts and save American lives.

We have asked a very limited number of individuals—visitors to our country holding passports from countries with active Al Qaeda operations—to speak voluntarily to law enforcement. We are forcing them to do nothing. We are merely asking them to do the right thing: to willingly disclose information they may have of terrorist threats to the lives and safety of all people in the United States. . . .

The Limits of Congress

We have worked with Congress in the belief and recognition that no single branch of government alone can stop terrorism. We have consulted with members out of respect for the separation of powers that is the basis of our system of government. However, Congress' power of oversight is not without limits. The Constitution specifically delegates to the President the authority to "take care that the laws are faithfully executed." And perhaps most importantly, the Constitution vests the President with the extraordinary and sole authority as Commander-in-Chief to lead our nation in times of war.

Mr. Chairman and members of the committee, not long ago I had the privilege of sitting where you now sit. I have the greatest reverence and respect for the constitutional responsibilities you shoulder. I will continue to consult with Congress so that you may fulfill your constitutional responsibilities. In some areas, however, I cannot and will not consult you. . . .

As Attorney General, it is my responsibility—at the direction of the President—to exercise those core executive powers the Constitution so designates. The law enforcement initiatives undertaken by the Department of Justice, those individuals we arrest, detain or seek to interview, fall under these core executive powers. In addition, the President's authority to establish war-crimes commissions arises out of his power as Commander in Chief. For centuries, Congress has recognized this authority and the Supreme Court has never held that any Congress may limit it.

In accordance with over two hundred years of historical and legal precedent, the executive branch is now exercising its core Constitutional powers in the interest of saving the lives of Americans. I trust that Congress will respect the proper limits of Executive Branch consultation that I am duty-bound to uphold. I trust, as well, that Congress will respect this President's authority to wage war on terrorism and defend our nation and its citizens with all the power vested in him by the Constitution and entrusted to him by the American people.

The Patriot Act Compromises Civil Liberties

Susan Herman

The Constitution of the United States separates the federal government into three branches: the executive, legislative, and judicial. Each branch has the authority to act on its own, but also the authority to regulate the other two branches. This system is known as "checks and balances" and is intended to ensure that no individual branch may abuse its power. The primary goal of the checks and balances system is the protection of the civil rights of the population.

When the Congress passed the USA Patriot Act in October 2001, critics argued that the balance between protecting civil rights and the law enforcement powers of the government had tipped dangerously toward unrestrained government tyranny. In the following essay, law professor Susan Herman argues that this unbalancing has granted the legislative branch, the U.S. Department of Justice, and the President himself the ability to make a variety of unilateral decisions unencumbered by the obligation to make such decisions public or to justify them. The most controversial of these new provisions is the right of federal agencies to search private property without notifying the suspect that the search has taken place, the increased ability to spy on telephone and internet communications, and the right to detain and deport non-citizens. Herman argues that these provisions unnecessarily extend the legislative branch's powers and that their supposed necessity in the war against terror remains unproven.

Until Attorney General Ashcroft finally agreed to appear before Congress [in December 2001] to report on the status of the domestic war against terrorism, rumors flew.

Susan Herman, "The USA Patriot Act and the US Department of Justice: Losing Our Balances?" *Jurist*, December 3, 2001. Reproduced by permission.

Various reporters speculated about how many people were in detention [in relation to the terrorist attacks of September 11, 2001 and the subsequent war in Afghanistan], how many as material witnesses, and how many for immigration violations. There have been rumors about deplorable conditions, coercive tactics, and failure to report the detention of certain foreign nationals to their consulates. Formal Freedom of Information Act requests for information were denied.

Ashcroft has now provided some information about numbers of detainees, but not names, and not the quality of evidence in the individual cases. He has confirmed the rumor that some suspects, in New York, are being held under seal. He has also affirmed that the detentions are of people suspected of being terrorists, and that the detentions have prevented terrorist acts. At least one federal judge in New York, looking at the evidence in a particular case, ordered that one of the detainees be released on bail, given that the evidence against him tended to show not that he was a terrorist, but that he had lied to a grand jury. To expressions of doubt, or requests for additional information, Ashcroft reaffirms more loudly that he is detaining terrorists, that arose detained would otherwise have committed terrorist acts, and that to share any more information than he has already shared with us or with Congress would aid Osama bin Laden [the leader of the al-Qaeda network responsible for the September 11 attacks] in his anti-American campaign. The message is simple: we must stop asking questions and just trust the Department of Justice to do the right thing. . . .

The Balance of Power

Partly because of the most recent spate of anti-terrorism legislation, two out of three branches of the federal government are also being left out of the loop in a growing number of circumstances. In its October USA Patriot Act [an eye-popping acronym for "Uniting and Strengthening America by Providing Appropriate Tools Required to Intercept and Obstruct Terrorism"], as in its September Use of Military Force Authorization, Congress has been consistently funneling power to the President and his Executive branch subordinates, while minimizing its own role, as well as the role of the judiciary, in the decisions that are to be made about the conduct of our foreign as well as our domestic war. The depth and breadth of the delegation of war powers is apparent on the face of the September 18 enactment, authorizing the President to "use all necessary and appropriate force against those nations, organizations, or persons he determines planned, authorized, committed, or aided the terrorist attacks that occurred on September 11, 2001, or harbored such organization or persons. . . ." Under this authorization, could the President simply decide to extend the war from Afghanistan to Iraq, Saudi Arabia, or even Germany without any further input from Congress? If Congress does not maintain an active role (as it reserves some option to do under the War Powers Resolution), the judiciary is unlikely to intervene, and the voting public only knows what the government tells us, where is the check?

It is less obvious how the balance of power has been shifted in the domestic war against terrorism because the provisions of the enormous USA Patriot Act are only the tip of an iceberg of amended legislation. Most of its provisions amend previous law by adding or deleting words, paragraphs, or sections, forcing people reading the legislation to embark on an elaborate treasure hunt, tracking each amendment back to try to determine its impact on the previous law. In addition, it is difficult to comprehend the new changes if one is not already conversant with labyrinthine webs of law in many different areas.

Here are a few examples of how the new legislation continues to force feed power to the executive branch, while limiting the judiciary, and keeping Congress in the dark.

Surveillance Provisions

The thrust of the USA Patriot Act surveillance provisions is to provide federal agencies with more surveillance options, and less judicial supervision. The principal statute governing electronic surveillance in criminal investigations, Title III of the Crime Control and Safe Streets Act of 1968, tried to meet concerns the Supreme Court had expressed about the constitutionality of electronic surveillance under Fourth Amendment, by providing standards to limit the scope of surveillance and by providing a judicial check. Except in certain cases deemed emergencies, applicants must persuade a judicial officer that they have probable cause that the interception they seek may provide evidence of one of a number of listed offenses. The court order permitting surveillance, like the statute, will require investigators to submit to various forms of limitations and judicial supervision. Evidence intercepted in violation of Title III's central provisions, which include a requirement that intrusions into conversations be "minimized," is made inadmissible in judicial and other proceedings. Cases decided in response to defendants' motions to suppress evidence seized then flesh out the nature of judicial participation.

The Foreign Intelligence Surveillance Act of 1978 [FISA], on the other hand, was aimed not at gathering evidence for a criminal prosecution, but at gathering information about the activities of foreign persons and agents (as opposed to "U.S. persons"). Judicial involvement in deciding whether to issue orders permitting this type of surveillance is both covert and minimal. Instead of requiring probable cause, surveillance orders are issued on a certification by the Attorney General that has nothing to do with probable cause. Between 1996 and 2000, out of 4,275 applications for FISA warrants, 4,275 were granted. Because the point is to gather intelligence rather than evidence, challenges to the legality of surveillance aren't likely to arise. The subjects may never even know that they have been under surveillance. . . .

Authority already existed for the government to order a telephone company to turn over a list of the numbers being dialed to and from a particular telephone, on a standard less than probable cause. If the government certifies that the information sought is "relevant to an ongoing criminal investigation," a judge "must" grant the order, regardless of whether or not the judge agrees with the government's conclusion, and even if the judge thinks the government is fishing. This ample authority, on the same unexamined certification, is now extended to trap and trace orders providing access to "dialing, routing and signaling information" in connection with computers. These terms are not defined (and are certainly not clear to a technologically challenged person like me), but seem to allow the government access to lists of E mails sent and received, as well as a list of the websites visited on a particular computer. In the telephone context, getting a "pen register," with its list of telephone numbers to and from which calls were made on a particular phone, offered no opportunity to hear the contents of those conversations. In the computer context, the information about E mail addresses and websites evidently travels with its content. The Department of Justice promises to separate the two and not pry into content. There seems to be no way of supervising whether this promise is kept. In addition, it seems that if a target uses a computer in a cyber café or the public library to check E mail or visit a website, surveillance of that computer may simply continue, giving the government access to the E mail and Internet activities of a multitude of non-targets.

Executive Prerogative

Most of the new surveillance powers granted will expire after four years pursuant to the statutes' sunset provisions.[1] Most of

1. Unable to reach agreement Congress extended the sunset provisions until March 2006 when it agreed to make 14 of 16 temporary provisions permanent and set four-year expirations on the other two.

the powers are not confined to investigations concerning terrorism, but apply to any criminal investigations. If there is to be any check on the Attorney General's use of these powers, it will have to come from congressional oversight. Will Congress be able to muster the political will to hold effective hearings, and to overcome the Bush Administration's reluctance to share what it claims as executive prerogative?

The USA Patriot Act also further increases the authority of the Attorney General to detain and deport non-citizens with little or no judicial review. The Attorney General may certify that he has "reasonable grounds to believe" that a non-citizen endangers national security. The Attorney General and Secretary of State are also given the authority to designate domestic groups as terrorist organizations, and deport any non-citizen who belongs to them. . . .

In addition to collecting the various powers described above, the Attorney General announced that he intends to eavesdrop on inmates' attorney-client conversations. He also announced plans to have state and local law enforcement officials cooperate in questioning 5,000 people, who appear to have been selected according to their ethnicity or religion. He acted to expand his power to detain immigrants, and to contract the information available under the Freedom of Information Act. . . .

Checks and Balances

Of course, I know the arguments in favor of granting the Attorney General and President the powers said to be necessary to keep us safe. Some of the more vocal members of Congress have been congratulating themselves for having struck an appropriate balance between our need for security and our need for civil liberties. But their balance was struck on the face of the legislation by confiding the critical decisions to the President, the Attorney General, and other Executive Branch officials. The avidity with which the Attorney General and President have shown themselves willing to make dramatic unilateral decisions does not reassure me about the existence of balance, or of checks. And how will we ever be able to evaluate whether or not the powers now wielded by the Executive Branch are, as the legislation asserts, "required" to combat terrorism? We may be selling our birthright for a mess of pottage.

My general level of trust in the government is conditioned on the existence of the Constitution's elaborate structure of checks and balances: the hydraulic pressures among the three branches of the federal government, the dialectic of federalism and the ultimate political power of an informed electorate. Now, there increasingly often seems to be only one locus of power. Increasingly often, the other two branches, the other axis of government (the states), and the electorate, including me, are asked not to know, but just to trust.

Three Strikes Laws Are Too Tough

Scott Ehlers, Vincent Schiraldi, and Jason Ziedenberg

In November 1995 Leandro Andrade, a U.S. Army veteran and heroin addict, attempted to shoplift a number of videotapes at a local Kmart store. The tapes, including Cinderella, Free Willie 2, *and* Snow White *were intended as Christmas presents for his nieces. He was apprehended by the store's security guards, but two weeks later he again attempted to steal the videotapes and was caught again. As punishment for these crimes Andrade was sentenced to fifty-years-to-life in prison, twenty-five years for each attempted petty theft. The severity of the punishment was the result of California's three strikes laws which state that when a person commits a third crime after having committed two prior felonies the sentence becomes a mandatory twenty-five-years-to-life. Although more than half of the nation's states have enacted three strikes laws, California's version is unique in that the third "strike" can be any misdemeanour crime and does not have to be violent or serious. Andrade had two prior convictions for home burglaries committed in 1983, though none of his crimes involved violence or weapons. Although critics of the law argued that Andrade's crime, which amounted to $153.54 worth of videotapes, did not justify such a harsh sentence. On March 5, 2003, the U.S. Supreme Court held by a 5-4 majority that such sentences were fair and constitutionally legal, and rejected Andrade's claim that they represented "cruel and unusual" punishment.*

In the following report published on the tenth anniversary of California's three strikes law, the Justice Policy Institute, a nonprofit research and public policy organization which advocates

Scott Ehlers, Vincent Schiraldi, and Jason Ziedenberg, *Still Striking Out: Ten Years of California's Three Strikes Law.* Washington, DC: Justice Policy Institute, 2004. www.justicepolicy.org/reports/threestrikes-9.04%20arial.doc. Reproduced by permission.

alternatives to prison, argues that California's 1994 law should be abolished as it does not effectively deter crime, does not target violent offenders, disproportionately incarcerates African Americans and Latinos, and is far too costly. In response to findings published in reports such as this, Californians were invited to vote on Proposition 66 in November 2004. The proposition would amend the three strikes law to require that the second and third strikes be either violent or serious felonies for the mandatory longer sentences to apply. Proponents argued that the amendment would restore the three strikes law to its original intent, the permanent incarceration of violent and serious offenders. Critics of the proposition argued that it would mean that up to 26,000 convicted felons would be released from prison. The proposition failed to pass.

March 7, 2004, marks the ten-year anniversary of the signing of AB 971, California's "Three Strikes and You're Out" law. In November 1994, California voters approved a ballot initiative that was virtually identical, except for one critical difference—the initiative required a vote of the people to alter the law, or a two-thirds vote of the Assembly and Senate.

While other states passed habitual offender laws in the early-to-mid-nineties, California's "Three Strikes" law was much more punitive—and far-reaching—in a number of respects. While other states' "Three Strikes" laws only applied to serious or violent offenses, California's required sentences to be doubled for *any* felony, if the offender had one prior serious or violent felony conviction on their record, or a 25-year-to-life sentence for *any* felony if the offender had two prior serious or violent felony convictions. In addition, persons convicted under the law were not eligible for parole until they served 80 percent of their sentence, while many other prisoners could be paroled after serving 50 percent of their time.

Since the passage of Three Strikes, tens of thousands of persons have been sentenced under the law in California, while a small fraction of that have been sentenced in other states. As an example, today over 42,000 persons—over one-in-four prisoners—are serving a doubled or 25-years-to-life sentence under the California law. As of June 2002, 5,837 offenders (12.5 percent) were serving prison sentences under Georgia's law. In Washington State, where voters approved the first Three Strikes law in 1993, 260 persons are in prison under the law today.

California's law is also different in another respect—it has generated more questions about the policy impact and effect of the law. Are most 'strikers'—persons serving a prison sentence under a second or third strike—incarcerated for violent behavior? Has the law reduced crime? Has the law led to large increases in prisoners—and taxpayer expenditures on prisons? Is Three Strikes the most cost-effective way to reduce crime? This report will address many of these same questions—10 years after the law came into effect. . . .

A Growing Prison Population

After the Three Strikes law passed, researchers and analysts predicted significant growth in California's prison population—and huge costs to the taxpayers to pay for it. The California Department of Corrections originally projected that the law would result in an additional 80,000 prisoners in the population by 1999, bringing the total prison population to 245,000. RAND [a policy think tank] estimated that the law would cost taxpayers an extra $4.5 billion to $6.5 billion *per year*. Luckily for California taxpayers, neither prediction came true because "the law has not been applied with 'full implementation,'" as expected by the Department of Corrections and RAND. Over time, prosecutors and judges have used their discretion to dismiss prior strikes, and the voters passed Proposition 36, the Substance Abuse and Crime Prevention Act, in the 2000 elections. Prop. 36 required drug possession offenders, including Three-Strikes-eligible offenders who have been out of prison for five years, to be eligible for drug treatment instead of being incarcerated. These two factors have slowed the pace of incarceration under the law.

While there may not be as many "strikers" in the prison population as originally projected, the law has still resulted in more people serving much longer sentences. . . . The California prison population grew from 125,473 in 1994, to 153,783 in June 2003, a 22.6 percent increase. An increasingly larger part of that population is made up of people serving a second or third strike. . . .

Little Impact on Crime

One of the key policy questions surrounding the Three Strikes law is whether or not it reduces crime, either by keeping repeat offenders in prison for longer periods of time (incapacitation) or by deterring would-be offenders from committing crimes out of fear of the longer sentences (deterrence). Over the last 10 years, researchers have tested these theories in a number of different ways, including by comparing jurisdictions within California, as well as comparing California's crime rate to that of other states around the country.

Peter Greenwood, former director of the RAND Corporation's Criminal Justice Program, recently summarized research findings around the impact of the Three Strikes law on crime rates:

> "Stolzenberg and D'Alessio (1997) analyzed serious crime trends in California's ten largest cities, using monthly data for 1985–1995. Their analysis suggests that the three strikes law did not reduce the California Crime Index below the level that would have been expected given the prevailing downward trend that had begun before the implementation of the law." *Journal of Crime and Delinquency*.

> "Macallair and Males (1999) and Austin et al. (1999) compared the crime rates of California counties that applied the law at higher and lower rates, expecting that counties with

more extensive three strikes enforcement should experience a larger drop in crime than those less likely to invoke the law. Both studies suggest no clear pattern of crime reduction associated with the rate of three strikes application." *Stanford Law and Policy Review.*

"A simulation study by Auerhahn (2001) suggests that the three strikes law has not made California streets safer. If a selective incapacitation policy is successful, 'dangerousness' should be maximized in the incarceration population and minimized in the rest of the population. Her analysis shows that the three strikes law has not been particularly successful in the selective incapacitation of dangerous offenders (a primary motivation for the law); the average dangerousness of the prison population has declined and that of the rest of the population has increased." *State University of New York Press.*

A subsequent policy question is, why has Three Strikes not had the impact on crime that its proponents thought it would? One explanation is that strikers account for relatively little crime, violent or otherwise. As Prof. Franklin Zimring and his colleagues point out in their book, *Punishment and Democracy: Three Strikes and You're Out in California,* even if all arrestees who met the criteria under the Three Strikes law "were to disappear from the earth without a trace," only 10.6 percent of felony crimes would be avoided.

CHAPTER 3

Punishing Crime

Chapter Preface

Shortly after sunrise on August 14, 1936, a young black man named Rainy Bethea, convicted for the rape and murder of a seventy-year-old woman, was hanged in what was to become the last public execution in America. The execution, held in Owensboro, Kentucky, was attended by some twenty-thousand people, with many travelling from out of state to witness the event. The raucous spectacle that attended the hanging helped to convince legislators that executions should not be open to the public.

At the time, there was a movement to make executions more humane, and many states had already adopted the electric chair as an alternative to hanging. First used in 1890, the electric chair soon became the prevalent form of state executions, replaced by most states in the 1980s by lethal injection, itself considered a more humane option. However, a controversial study published in 2005 raised questions about the humaneness of lethal injection, leading to the ongoing postponement of a number of executions in 2006. Although the methods used for administering the punishment of death have proved controversial, these issues pale when compared to the intense debate that has surrounded America's continued application of capital punishment.

Although capital punishment has been practiced in nearly all societies at some time, the United States remains unique among Western industrialized nations today in retaining the use of death as punishment. The issue has long divided Americans, but surveys have consistently reported that a majority support capital punishment, with the exception of a period during the 1950s and 1960s. Proponents argue that capital punishment is justified by the principle of retribution; that is, some crimes are so severe that the only just punishment is death. Opponents argue that life imprisonment is an effective substitute, that capital punishment regularly leads to irreversible miscarriages of justice, and that death sentences are often applied arbitrarily.

However, what underlies both claims is the principle that the punishment meted out by the criminal justice system should be proportional to the crime. While this idea has always informed the legal system, a variety of twentieth-century debates have demonstrated that designing proportional punishment is no simple matter. One such debate was sparked by New York State's 1973 decision to introduce mandatory-minimum sentences of fifteen-years-to-life imprisonment for possession of relatively small amounts of drugs. While some argue that mandatory-minimum sentences ensure uniformity in sentencing, opponents argue that such laws do not take into account the circumstances of the criminal and the crime and inevitably lead to disproportional sentences.

Another debate concerning the proportionality of punishments was sparked during the 1980s by attempts to increase punishments for criminal acts that were determined to be motivated by hatred for minority groups. Supporters argue that because such acts are directed not only toward the victims but all the members of the group to which the victim belongs, they deserved tougher punishments. Others argue that the increased penalties imposed by hate-crime legislation represent disproportional punishment insofar as they criminalize motives rather than actions.

Further complicating the issue of proportional punishment was the wave of corporate scandals that surfaced in 2002. Historically, white-collar crime has been understood to be less significant than the crimes collectively known as street crime, but the public's growing awareness of the incidence of corporate crime and its impact (a number of these scandals involved fraud valued at billions of dollars, not to mention the livelihoods of thousands of employees) led many to call for tougher punishments for white-collar criminals. In cases such as these, determining an appropriate punishment has proved a controversial and difficult task.

The Death Penalty is Unjust and Ineffective

Cesare Bonesana Marchese di Beccaria

In 1764 an Italian nobleman named Cesare Bonesana Marchese di Beccaria published a treatise titled On Crimes and Punishments, *which advocated a rationalist reform of Italy's criminal justice system. Beccaria originally published the work anonymously fearing a political backlash, but it quickly achieved widespread popularity and he subsequently had it published under his own name. It is difficult to overstate the impact it had on the reform of penal systems across Europe where it was praised by the Empress of Russia Catherine the Great and the French writer Voltaire, and in America where it was quoted by U.S. presidents John Adams and Thomas Jefferson.*

In addition to developing a number of rational punishment principles, such as punishment had a preventative not a retributive function, criminal processes should be public, and punishment should be proportionate to the crime committed, Beccaria's book also provides one of the first published arguments against the death penalty. Beccaria opposes the death penalty on two grounds. First, he argues that the state does not possess the right to take lives. According to Beccaria, the social contract does not allow for the taking of a life and that it is an absurdity that the same system that prohibits homicide should condemn people to die. Second, he asserts that capital punishment does not successfully deter crime. Instead he argues that long term imprisonment is a more powerful deterrent. While execution provides a single shocking example of punishment, it is transient, and "perpetual slavery," or long term imprisonment, provides the spectator with a longer lasting impression and is therefore a more influential tool for correcting criminal behavior.

Cesare Bonesana Marchese di Beccaria, from *Of Crimes and Punishments*. Translated by Edward D. Ingraham. Philadelphia: Philip H. Nicklin, 1819. Originally published in Italian in 1764.

The useless profusion of punishments, which has never made men better induces me to inquire, whether the punishment of death be really just or useful in a well governed state? What right, I ask, have men to cut the throats of their fellow-creatures? Certainly not that on which the sovereignty and laws are founded. The laws ... are only the sum of the smallest portions of the private liberty of each individual, and represent the general will, which is the aggregate of that of each individual. Did any one ever give to others the right of taking away his life? Is it possible that, in the smallest portions of the liberty of each, sacrificed to the good of the public, can be contained the greatest of all good, life? If it were so, how shall it be reconciled to the maxim which tells us, that a man has no right to kill himself, which he certainly must have, if he could give it away to another?

But the punishment of death is not authorised by any right; for I have demonstrated that no such right exists. It is therefore a war of a whole nation against a citizen whose destruction they consider as necessary or useful to the general good. But if I can further demonstrate that it is neither necessary nor useful, I shall have gained the cause of humanity....

A Momentary Spectacle

It is not the intenseness of the pain that has the greatest effect on the mind, but its continuance; for our sensibility is more easily and more powerfully affected by weak but repeated impressions, than by a violent but momentary impulse. The power of habit is universal over every sensible being. As it is by that we learn to speak, to walk, and to satisfy our necessities, so the ideas of morality are stamped on our minds by repeated impression. The death of a criminal is a terrible but momentary spectacle, and therefore a less efficacious method of deterring others than the continued example of a man deprived of his liberty, condemned, as a beast of burden, to repair, by his labour, the injury he has done to society. If I com-

155

mit such a crime, says the spectator to himself, I shall be reduced to that miserable condition for the rest of my life. A much more powerful preventive than the fear of death which men always behold in distant obscurity.

The terrors of death make so slight an impression, that it has not force enough to withstand the forgetfulness natural to mankind, even in the most essential things, especially when assisted by the passions. Violent impressions surprise us, but their effect is momentary; they are fit to produce those revolutions which instantly transform a common man into a Lacedaemonian or a Persian; but in a free and quiet government they ought to be rather frequent than strong.

The execution of a criminal is to the multitude a spectacle which in some excites compassion mixed with indignation. These sentiments occupy the mind much more than that salutary terror which the laws endeavor to inspire; but, in the contemplation of continued suffering, terror is the only, or at least predominant sensation. The severity of a punishment should be just sufficient to excite compassion in the spectators, as it is intended more for them than for the criminal.

Perpetual Slavery

A punishment, to be just, should have only that degree of severity which is sufficient to deter others. Now there is no man who upon the least reflection, would put in competition the total and perpetual loss of his liberty, with the greatest advantages he could possibly obtain in consequence of a crime. Perpetual slavery, then, has in it all that is necessary to deter the most hardened and determined, as much as the punishment of death. I say it has more. There are many who can look upon death with intrepidity and firmness, some through fanaticism, and others through vanity, which attends us even to the grave; others from a desperate resolution, either to get rid of their misery, or cease to live: but fanaticism and vanity forsake the criminal in slavery, in chains and fetters, in an iron cage, and despair seems rather the beginning than the end of their misery. The mind, by collecting itself and uniting all its force, can, for a moment, repel assailing grief; but its most vigorous efforts are insufficient to resist perpetual wretchedness.

In all nations, where death is used as a punishment, every example supposes a new crime committed; whereas, in perpetual slavery, every criminal affords a frequent and lasting example; and if it be necessary that men should often be witnesses of the power of the laws, criminals should often be put to death: but this supposes a frequency of crimes; and from hence this punishment will cease to have its effect, so that it must be useful and useless at the same time.

I shall be told that perpetual slavery is as painful a punishment as death, and therefore as cruel. I answer, that if all the miserable moments in the life of a slave were collected into one point, it would be a more cruel punishment than any other; but these are scattered through his whole life, whilst the pain of death exerts all its force in a moment. There is also another advantage in the punishment of slavery, which is, that it is more terrible to the spectator than to the sufferer himself; for the spectator considers the sum of all his wretched moments whilst the sufferer, by the misery of the present, is prevented from thinking of the future. All evils are increased by the imagination, and the sufferer finds resources and consolations of which the spectators are ignorant, who judge by their own sensibility of what passes in a mind by habit grown callous to misfortune. . . .

Punishment in a Just Society

He who foresees that he must pass a great number of years, even his whole life, in pain and slavery, a slave to those laws by which he, was protected, in sight of his fellow-citizens, with whom he lives in freedom and society, makes a useful comparison between those evils, the uncertainty of his success, and the shortness of the time in which he shall enjoy the fruits of his transgression. The example of those wretches, continually before his eyes, makes a much greater impression on him than a punishment, which instead of correcting, makes him more obdurate.

The punishment of death is pernicious to society, from the example of barbarity it affords. If the passions, or the necessity of war, have taught men to shed the blood of their fellow creatures, the laws, which are intended to moderate the ferocity of mankind, should not increase it by examples of barbarity, the more horrible as this punishment is usually attended with formal pageantry. Is it not absurd, that the laws, which detest and punish homicide, should, in order to prevent murder, publicly commit murder themselves? What are the true and most useful laws? Those compacts and conditions which all would propose and observe in those moments when private interest is silent, or combined with that of the public. What are the natural sentiments of every person concerning the punishment of death? We may read them in the contempt and indignation with which every one looks on the executioner, who is nevertheless an innocent executor of the public will, a good citizen, who contributes to the advantage of society, the instrument of the general security within, as good soldiers are without. What then is the origin of this contradiction? Why is this sentiment of mankind indelible to the scandal of reason? It is, that, in a secret corner of the mind, in which the original impressions of nature are still preserved, men discover a sentiment which tells them, that their lives are not lawfully in the power of any one, but of that necessity only which with its iron sceptre rules the universe.

What must men think, when they see wise magistrates and grave ministers of justice, with indifference and tranquillity, dragging a criminal to death, and whilst a wretch trembles with agony, expecting the fatal stroke, the judge, who has condemned him, with the coldest insensibility, and perhaps with no small gratification from the exertion of his authority, quits his tribunal, to enjoy the comforts and pleasures of life? They will say, "Ah! Those cruel formalities of justice are a cloak to tyranny, they are a secret language, a solemn veil, intended to conceal the sword by which we are sacrificed to the insatiable idol of despotism. Murder, which they would represent to us a horrible crime, we see practised by them without repugnance or remorse. Let us follow their example. A violent death appeared terrible in their descriptions, but we see that it is the affair of a moment. It will be still less terrible to him who, not expecting it, escapes almost all the pain." Such is the fatal though absurd reasonings of men who are disposed to commit crimes, on whom the abuse of religion has more influence than religion itself.

End the Death Penalty

If it be objected, that almost all nations in all ages have punished certain crimes with death, I answer, that the force of these examples vanishes when opposed to truth, against which prescription is urged in vain. The history of mankind is an immense sea of errors, in which a few obscure truths may here and there be found.

But human sacrifices have also been common in almost all nations. That some societies only it either few in number, or for a very short time, abstained from the punishment of death, is rather favourable to my argument; for such is the fate of great truths, that their duration is only as a flash of lightning in the long and dark night of error. The happy time is not yet arrived, when truth, as falsehood has been hitherto, shall be the portion of the greatest number.

The Penitentiary System
Should Rehabilitate Criminals

Gustave de Beaumont and Alexis de Tocqueville

In May 1831 two young Frenchmen, Alexis de Tocqueville and Gustave de Beaumont, arrived in Newport, Rhode Island. Their goal was to travel the United States and to study its penitentiary system in order to produce a report on prison reform in France. Beaumont and Tocqueville spent nine months travelling throughout America, going as far west as Michigan and south to New Orleans, interviewing prisoners and prison officials in an effort to determine the ideal penitentiary system. The two men believed that the rehabilitation of criminals into productive citizens was in the best interest of society and that the intelligent design of a penitentiary system could achieve this goal. To this end they strongly opposed the harsh punishments regularly meted out to offenders at the time.

What Beaumont and Tocqueville found in their travels was that the United States contained both the best and the worst examples of penitentiaries. The worst penitentiaries were those that locked up prisoners in inhumane conditions, imposed barbaric treatment, and made no effort to rehabilitate criminals. The best system was that found in Pennsylvania; it was the result of a long experiment in prison reformation originally developed by the Quakers, and based on solitary confinement and silence. In the following article Beaumont and Tocqueville argue that solitary confinement is necessary in order to prevent harmful contact between prisoners, which would only encourage deviant behavior, but also to induce them to reflect on their crimes, which would ultimately lead to their rehabilitation. However, the authors caution that this system of solitary confinement could not

Gustave de Beaumont and Alexis de Tocqueville, *On the Penitentiary System in the United States and Its Application in France.* Translated by Francis Lieber. Carbondale, IL: Southern Illinois University Press, 1979. First published in 1833. Copyright © 1964 by Southern Illinois University Press. All rights reserved. Reproduced by permission.

be absolute because "absolute solitude, if nothing interrupts it, is beyond the strength of man; it destroys the criminal without intermission and without pity; it does not reform, it kills." With this in mind, the authors ultimately advocate for a novel system that confines prisoners to solitary cells at night and forces them to work during the day.

Though the penitentiary system in the United States is a new institution, its origin must be traced back to times already long gone by. The first idea of a reform in the American prisons, belongs to a religious sect in Pennsylvania. The Quakers, who abhor all shedding of blood, had always protested against the barbarous laws which the colonies inherited from their mother country. In 1786, their voice succeeded in finding due attention, and from this period, punishment of death, mutilation and the whip were successively abolished in almost all cases by the Legislature of Pennsylvania. A less cruel fate awaited the convicts from this period. The punishment of imprisonment was substituted for corporal punishment, and the law authorized the courts to inflict solitary confinement in a cell during day and night, upon those guilty of capital crimes. It was then that the Walnut Street prison was established in Philadelphia. Here the convicts were classed according to the nature of their crimes, and separate cells were constructed for those whom the courts of justice had sentenced to absolute isolation. These cells also served to curb the resistance of individuals, unwilling to submit to the discipline of the prison. The solitary prisoners did not work.

This innovation was good but incomplete. . . .

The Birth of the Penitentiary System

The impossibility of subjecting criminals to a useful classification, has since been acknowledged, and solitary confinement without labor has been condemned by experience. It is nevertheless just to say, that the trial of this theory has not been made long enough to be decisive. The authority given to the judges of Pennsylvania, by the law of April 5, 1790, and of March 22, to send criminals to the prison in Walnut Street, who formerly would have been sent to the different county jails, soon produced in this prison such a crowd of convicts, that the difficulty of classification increased in the same degree as the cells became insufficient.

To say the truth there did not yet exist a penitentiary system in the United States.

If it be asked why this name was given to the system of imprisonment which had been established, we would answer, that then as well as now, the abolition of the punishment of death was confounded in America, with the penitentiary system. People said—*instead of killing the guilty, our laws put them in prison; hence we have a penitentiary system.*

The conclusion was not correct. It is very true that the punishment of death applied to the greater part of crimes, is irreconcilable with a system of imprisonment; but this punishment abolished, the penitentiary system does not yet necessarily exist; it is further necessary, that the criminal whose life has been spared, be placed in a prison, whose discipline renders him better. Because, if the system, instead of reforming, should only tend to corrupt him still more, this would not be any longer a penitentiary system, but only a bad system of imprisonment.

This mistake of the Americans has for a long time been shared in France. In 1794, the Duke de la Rochefoucauld-Liancourt, published an interesting notice on the prison of Philadelphia: he declared that this city had an excellent prison system, and all the world repeated it.

A Flawed Experiment

However, the Walnut Street prison could produce none of the effects which are expected from this system. It had two principal faults: it corrupted by contamination those who worked together. It corrupted by indolence, the individuals who were plunged into solitude.

The true merit of its founders was the abolition of the sanguinary laws of Pennsylvania, and by introducing a new system of imprisonment, the direction of public attention to this important point. Unfortunately that which in this innovation deserved praise, was not immediately distinguished from that which was untenable.

Solitude applied to the criminal, in order to conduct him to reformation by reflection, rests upon a philosophical and true conception. But the authors of this theory had not yet founded its application upon those means which alone could render it practical and salutary. Yet their mistake was not immediately perceived, and the success of Walnut Street prison boasted of in the United States still more than in Europe, biased public opinion in favor of its faults, as well as its advantages.

An Inefficient System

The first state which showed itself zealous to imitate Pennsylvania, was that of New York, which in 1797, adopted both new penal laws and a new prison system.

Solitary confinement without labor, was admitted here as in Philadelphia, but, as in Walnut Street, it was reserved for those who especially were sentenced to undergo it by the courts of justice, and for those who opposed the established order of the prison. Solitary confinement, therefore, was not the ordinary system of the establishment; it awaited only those great criminals who, before the reform of the penal laws, would have been condemned to death. Those who were guilty of less offenses were put indiscriminately together in the prison. They, different from the inmates of the solitary cells, had to work during the day, and the only disciplinary punishment which their keeper had a right to inflict, in case of breach of the order of the prison, was solitary confinement, with bread and water.

The Walnut Street prison was imitated by others: Maryland, Massachusetts, Maine, New Jersey, Virginia, etc. Adopted successively, the principle of solitary confinement, applied only to a certain class of criminals in each of these states. The reform of criminal laws preceded that of the hoped-for success. In general it was ruinous to the public treasury; it never effected the reformation of the prisoners. Every year the legislature of each state voted considerable funds towards the support of the penitentiaries, and the continued return of the same individuals into the prisons proved the inefficiency of the system to which they were submitted.

Such results seem to prove the insufficiency of the whole system; however instead of accusing the theory itself, its execution was attacked. It was believed that the whole evil resulted from the paucity of cells, and the crowding of the prisoners; and that the system, such as it was established, would be fertile in happy results, if some new buildings were added to the prisons already existing. New expenses therefore, and new efforts were made.

A New Experiment in Prisons

Such was the origin of the Auburn prison [1816]. This prison, which has become so celebrated since, was at first founded upon a plan essentially erroneous. It limited itself to some classifications, and each of these cells was destined to receive two convicts: it was of all combinations the most unfortunate; it would have been better to throw together fifty criminals in the same room, than to separate them two by two. This inconvenience was soon felt, and in 1819 the Legislature of the State of New York, ordered the erection of a new building at Auburn (the northern wing) in order to increase the number of solitary cells. However, it must be observed, that no idea as yet existed of the system which has prevailed since. It was not intended to subject all the convicts to the system of cells, but its application was only to be made to a greater number. At the same time the same theories produced the same trials in Philadelphia, where the little success of the Walnut Street prison would have convinced the inhabitants of Pennsylvania of its inefficiency, if the latter, like the citizens of the State of New York, had not been led to seek in the faults of execution, a motive for allowing the principle to be correct.

In 1817, the Legislature of Pennsylvania decreed the erection of the penitentiary at Pittsburgh, for the western counties, and in 1821, that of the penitentiary of Cherry Hill, for the city of Philadelphia and the eastern counties.

The principles to be followed in the construction of these two establishments were, however, not entirely the same as those on which the Walnut Street prison had been erected. In the latter, classification formed the predominant system, to which solitary confinement was but secondary. In the new prisons the classifications were abandoned, and a solitary cell was to be prepared for each convict. The criminal was not to leave his cell day or night, and all labor was denied to him in his solitude. Thus absolute solitary confinement, which in Walnut Street was but accidental, was now to become the foundation of the system adopted for Pittsburgh and Cherry Hill.

The experiment which was to be made, promised to be decisive; no expense was spared to construct these new establishments worthy of their object, and the edifices which were elevated, resembled prisons less than palaces.

Solitary Confinement Kills

In the meantime, before even the laws which ordered their erection, were executed, the Auburn prison had been tried in the State of New York. Lively debates ensued on this occasion, in the legislature, and the public was impatient to know the result of the new trials, which had just been made.

The northern wing having been nearly finished in 1821, eighty prisoners were placed there, and a separate cell was given to each. This trial, from which so happy a result had been anticipated, was fatal to the greater part of the convicts. In order to reform them, they had been submitted to complete isolation; but this absolute solitude, if nothing interrupts it, is beyond the strength of man; it destroys the criminal without intermission and without pity; it does not reform, it kills.

The unfortunates, on whom this experiment was made, fell to a state of depression, so manifest, that their keepers are struck with it; their lives seemed in danger, if they remained longer in this situation; five of them, had already succumbed during a single year; their moral state was not less alarming; one of them had become insane; another, in a fit of despair, had embraced the opportunity when the keeper brought him something, to precipitate himself from his cell, running the almost certain chance of a mortal fall.

Upon similar effects the system was finally judged. The Governor of the State of New York pardoned twenty-six of those in solitary confinement; the others to whom this favor was not extended, were allowed to leave the cells during the day, and to work in the common workshops of the prison. From this period, (1823) the system of unmodified isolation ceased entirely to be practiced at Auburn. Proofs were soon afforded that this system, fatal to the health of the criminals, was likewise inefficient in producing their reform. Of twenty-six convicts, pardoned by the governor, fourteen returned a short time after into the prison, in consequence of new offenses.

The Ideal System

This experiment, so fatal to those who were selected to undergo it, was of a nature to endanger the success of the penitentiary system altogether. After the melancholy effects of isolation, it was to be feared that the whole principle would be rejected: it would have been a natural reaction. The Americans were wiser: the idea was not given up, that the solitude, which causes the criminal to reflect, exercises a beneficial influence; and the problem was, to find the means by which the evil effect of total solitude could be avoided without giving up its advantages. It was believed that this end could be attained, by leaving the convicts in their cells during night, and by making them work during the day, in the common workshops, obliging them at the same time to observe absolute silence. . . .

[Cherry Hill Prison in Pennsylvania] adopted a system which at once agreed with the austerity of her manners, and her philanthropical sensibility. She rejected solitude without labor, the fatal effects of which experience had proved everywhere, and she retained the absolute separation of the prisoners—a severe punishment, which, in order to be inflicted, needs not the support of corporal chastisement.

The penitentiary of Cherry Hill, founded on these principles, is therefore a combination of Pittsburgh and Auburn. Isolation during night and day, has been retained from the Pittsburgh system: and, into the solitary cell, the labor of Auburn has been introduced.

This revolution in the prison discipline of Pennsylvania, was immediately followed by a general reform of her criminal laws. All punishments were made milder; the severity of solitary imprisonment permitted an abridgment of its duration; capital punishment was abolished in all cases, except that of premeditated murder. . . .

The Ancient System

It would be wrong to judge all the United States by the picture which we have presented of the improvements adopted. . . .

In [many states], the ancient system prevails in its whole force; the crowding of prisoners, confusion of crimes, ages, and sometimes sexes, mixture of indicted and convicted prisoners, of criminals and debtors, guilty persons and witnesses; considerable mortality; frequent escapes; absence of all discipline, no silence which leads the criminals to reflection; no labor which accustoms them to an honest mode of subsistence; insalubrity of the place which destroys health; ignism of the conversations which corrupt; idleness that depraves; the assemblage, in one word, of all vices and all immoralities—such is the picture offered by the prisons which have not yet entered into the way of reform.

By the side of one state, the penitentiaries of which might serve as a model, we find another, whose jails present the example of everything which ought to be avoided. Thus the State of New York is without contradiction one of the most advanced in the path of reform, while New Jersey, which is separated from it but by a river, has retained all the vices of the ancient system.

Ohio, which possesses a penal code remarkable for the mildness and humanity of its provisions, has barbarous prisons. We have deeply sighed when at Cincinnati, visiting the prison. We found half of the imprisoned charged with irons, and the rest plunged into an infected dungeon; and are unable to describe the painful impression which we experienced, when, examining the prison of New Orleans, we found men together with hogs, in the midst of all odors and nuisances. In locking up the criminals, nobody thinks of rendering them better, but only of taming their malice; they are put in chains like ferocious beasts; and instead of being corrected, they are rendered brutal.

Mandatory Jail Sentencing Is Unfair

Lois G. Forer

For most of the twentieth century judges in the United States worked under an indeterminate sentencing system, which meant that they were largely responsible for determining the appropriate punishment for the guilty that stood before them. By the 1970s this system came under attack from attorneys, legislators, and scholars, who argued that it was a flawed system on two counts. First, it was unfair on criminals as it allowed the personal prejudices of judges to affect cases (for example, racist judges could impose harsher sentences on black criminals). Second, it was unfair on society as some judges were seen to impose sentences that were too lenient. In order to respond to these concerns Congress passed the Sentencing Reform Act of 1984, which was a set of sentencing guidelines which judges were required to follow, and made for a uniformity in sentencing. The guidelines reflected the "get tough on crime" attitude of its creators and favored harsher punishments and longer prison times for convicts.

In the following article, former Philadelphia judge Lois Forer argues that the mandatory sentencing law has not made the criminal system fairer; rather, it has created a system that is unfair because it does not take into account the individual circumstances of a crime. Forer also argues that the law is unconstitutional insofar as it violates the principle of separation of powers. But for Forer, the principal argument against the mandatory sentencing law is its readiness to incarcerate convicts rather than to devise more socially responsive sentences.

Lois G. Forer, "Justice by Numbers: Mandatory Sentencing Drove Me from the Bench," *Washington Monthly*, April 1, 1992. Copyright 1992 by Washington Monthly Publishing, LLC, 733 15th St. NW, Suite 520, Washington, DC 20005. (202) 393–5155. Web site: www.washingtonmonthly.com. Reproduced by permission.

Michael S. would have been one of the more than 600,000 incarcerated persons in the United States. He would have been a statistic, yet another addition to a clogged criminal justice system. But he's not—in part because to me Michael was a human being: a slight twenty-four-year-old with a young wife and small daughter. Not that I freed him; I tried him and found him guilty. He is free now only because he is a fugitive. I have not seen him since the day of his sentencing in 1984, yet since that day our lives have been inextricably connected. Because of his case I retired from the bench.

Michael's case appeared routine. He was a typical offender: young, black, and male, a high-school dropout without a job. The charge was an insignificant holdup that occasioned no comment in the press. And the trial itself was, in the busy life of a judge, a run-of-the-mill event.

An Unconstitutional Penalty

The year before, Michael, brandishing a toy gun, held up a taxi and took $50 from the driver and the passenger, harming neither. This was Michael's first offense. Although he had dropped out of school to marry his pregnant girlfriend, Michael later obtained a high school equivalency diploma. He had been steadily employed, earning enough to send his daughter to parochial school—a considerable sacrifice for him and his wife. Shortly before the holdup, Michael had lost his job. Despondent because he could not support his family, he went out on a Saturday night, had more than a few drinks, and then robbed the taxi.

There was no doubt that Michael was guilty. But the penalty posed problems. To me, a robbery in a taxi is not an intrinsically graver offense than a robbery in an alley, but to the Pennsylvania legislature, it is. Because the holdup occurred on public transportation, it fell within the ambit of the state's mandatory sentencing law—which required a minimum sentence of five years in the state penitentiary. In Pennsylvania, a prosecutor may decide not to demand imposition of that law, but Michael's prosecuting attorney wanted the five-year sentence.

One might argue that a five-year sentence for a $50 robbery is excessive or even immoral, but to a judge, those arguments are necessarily irrelevant. He or she has agreed to enforce the law, no matter how ill-advised, unless the law is unconstitutional.

I believed the mandatory sentencing law was, and like many of my colleagues I had held it unconstitutional in several other cases for several reasons. We agreed that it violates the constitutional principle of separation of powers because it can be invoked by the prosecutor, and not by the judge. In addition, the act is arbitrary and capricious in its application. Robbery, which is often a simple purse snatching, is covered, but not child molestation or incest, two of society's most damaging offenses. Nor can a defendant's previous record or mental state be considered. A hardened repeat offender receives the same sentence as a retarded man who steals out of hunger. Those facts violate the fundamental Anglo-American legal principles of individualized sentencing and proportionality of the penalty to the crime.

Thus in Michael's case, I again held the statute to be unconstitutional and turned to the sentencing guidelines—a state statute designed to give uniform sentences to offenders who commit similar crimes. The minimum sentence prescribed by the guidelines was twenty-four months.

An Alternative Sentence

A judge can deviate from the prescribed sentence if he or she writes an opinion explaining the reasons for the deviation. While this sounds reasonable in theory, "downwardly departing" from the guidelines is extremely difficult. The mitigating circumstances that influence most judges are not included in the limited list of factors on which "presumptive" sentence is based—that an offender is a caretaker of small children; that the offender is mentally retarded; or that the offender, like Michael, is emotionally distraught.

So I decided to deviate from the guidelines, sentencing Michael to eleven-and-a-half months in the county jail and permitting him to work outside the prison during the day to support his family. I also imposed a sentence of two years' probation following his imprisonment conditioned upon re-payment of the $50. My rationale for the lesser penalty, outlined in my lengthy opinion, was that this was a first offense, no one was harmed, Michael reacted under the pressures of unemployment and need, and he seemed truly contrite. He had never committed a violent act and posed no danger to the public. A sentence of close to a year seemed adequate to convince Michael of the seriousness of his crime. Nevertheless, the prosecutor appealed.

Michael returned to his family, obtained steady employment, and repaid the victims of his crime. I thought no more about Michael until 1986, when the state supreme court upheld the appeal and ordered me to resentence him to a minimum of five years in the state penitentiary. By this time Michael had successfully completed his term of imprisonment and probation, including payment of restitution. I checked Michael's record. He had not been rearrested.

I was faced with a legal and moral dilemma. As a judge I had sworn to uphold the law, and I could find no legal grounds for violating an order of the supreme court. Yet five years' imprisonment was grossly disproportionate to the offense. The usual grounds for imprisonment are retribution, deterrence, and rehabilitation. Michael had paid his retribution by a short term of imprisonment and by making restitution to the victims. He had been effectively deterred from committing future crimes. And by any measurable standard he had been rehabilitated. There was no social or criminological justification for sending him back to prison. Given the choice between defying a court order or my conscience, I decided to leave the bench where I had sat for sixteen years.

Mandatory Sentencing Ignores the Human Being Involved

That didn't help Michael, of course; he was resentenced by another judge to serve the balance of the five years: four years and fifteen days. Faced with this prospect, he disappeared. A bench warrant was issued, but given the hundreds of fugitives—including dangerous ones—loose in Philadelphia, I doubt that anyone is seriously looking for him.

But any day he may be stopped for a routine traffic violation; he may apply for a job or a license; he may even be the victim of a crime—and if so, the ubiquitous computer will be alerted and he will be returned to prison to serve the balance of his sentence, plus additional time for being a fugitive. It is not a happy prospect for him and his family—nor for America, which is saddled with a punishment system that operates like a computer—crime in, points tallied, sentence out— utterly disregarding the differences among the human beings involved.

The mandatory sentencing laws and guidelines that exist today in every state were designed to smooth out the inequities in the American judiciary, and were couched in terms of fairness to criminals—they would stop the racist judge from sentencing black robbers to be hanged, or the crusading judge from imprisoning pot smokers for life. Guidelines make sense, for that very reason. But they have had an ugly and unintended result—and increase in the number of American prisoners and an increase in the length of the sentences they serve. Meanwhile, the laws have effectively neutralized judges who prefer sentencing the nonviolent to alternative programs or attempt to keep mothers with young children out of jail.

Have the laws made justice fairer—the central objective of the law? I say no, and a [August 1991] report by the Federal

Sentencing Commission concurs. It found that, even under mandatory sentencing laws, black males served 83.4 months to white males' 53.7 months for the same offenses. (Prosecutors are more likely to demand imposition of the mandatory laws for blacks than for whites.)

Most important, however, as mandatory sentencing packs our prisons and busts our budgets, it doesn't prevent crime very effectively. For certain kinds of criminals, alternative sentencing is the most effective type of punishment. That, by the way, is a cold, hard statistic—rather like Michael will be when they find him. . . .

The Origins of Mandatory Sentencing

How did we get into this no-win situation? Like most legislative reforms, it started with good intentions. In 1970, after the turmoil of the sixties, legislators were bombarded with pleas for "law and order." A young, eager, newly appointed federal judge, Marvin Frankel, had an idea.

Before his appointment, Frankel had experienced little personal contact with the criminal justice system. Yet his slim book, *Fair and Certain Punishment*, offered a system of guidelines to determine the length of various sentences. Each crime was given a certain number of points. The offender was also given a number of points depending upon his or her prior record, use of a weapon, and a few other variables. The judge merely needed to add up the points to calculate the length of imprisonment.

The book was widely read and lauded for two main reasons. First, it got tough on criminals and made justice "certain." A potential offender would know in advance the penalty he would face and thus be deterred. (Of course, a large proportion of street crimes are not premeditated, but that fact was ignored.) And second, it got tough on the "bleeding heart" judges. All offenders similarly situated would be treated the same.

The plan sounded so fair and politically promising that many states rushed to implement it in the seventies. In Pennsylvania, members of the legislature admonished judges not to oppose the guidelines because the alternative would be even worse: mandatory sentences. In fact, within a few years almost every jurisdiction had both sentencing guidelines and mandatory sentencing laws. Since then. Congress has enacted some sixty mandatory sentencing laws on the federal level.

As for unfairnesses in sentencing—for instance, the fact that the robber with his finger in his jacket gets the same sentence as the guy with a semiautomatic—these could have been rectified by giving appellate courts jurisdiction to review sentences, as is the law in Canada. This was not done on either the state or federal level. Thus what influential criminologist James Q. Wilson had argued during the height of the battle had become the law of the land: The legal system should "most definitely stop pretending that the judges know any better than the rest of us how to provide 'individualized justice.'"

Individualized Justice

I'm not sure I knew better than the rest of you, but I knew a few things about Michael and the correctional system I would be throwing him into. At the time of Michael's sentencing, both the city of Philadelphia and the commonwealth of Pennsylvania were, like many cities and states, in such poor fiscal shape that they did not have money for schools and health care, let alone new prisons, and the one they did have were overflowing. The city was under a federal order to reduce the prison population; untried persons accused of dangerous crimes were being released, as were offenders who had not completed their sentences.

As for Michael, his problems and those of his family were very real to me. Unlike appellate judges who never see the individuals whose lives and property they dispose of, a trial judge sees living men and women. I had seen Michael and his wife and daughter. I had heard him express remorse. I had favorable reports about him from the prison and his parole officer. Moreover, Michael, like many offenders who appeared before me, had written to me several times. I felt I knew him.

Of course, I could have been wrong. As Wilson says, judges are not infallible—and most of them know that. But they have heard the evidence, seen the offender, and been furnished with presentence reports and psychiatric evaluations. They are in a better position to evaluate the individual and devise an appropriate sentence than anyone else in the criminal justice system.

Yet under mandatory sentencing laws, the complexities of each crime and criminal are ignored. And seldom do we ask what was once a legitimate question in criminal justice: What are the benefits of incarceration? The offenders are off the streets for the period of the sentence, but once released, most will soon be rearrested. (Many crimes are committed in prison, including murder, rape, robbery, and drug dealing.) They have not been "incapacitated," another of the theoretical justifications for imprisonment. More likely, they have simply been hardened.

Hate Is Not a Crime

James B. Jacobs

A little after midnight December 20, 1986, three black men were attacked in Brooklyn, New York, by a group of a dozen white men and boys with baseball bats shouting racial slurs. In an attempt to escape, one of the three men was struck by a car and killed when he ran onto the highway in an attempt to escape. While race-motivated crime has a long history in the United States, the coverage and analysis that followed this incident created the political agenda for the creation of hate crime laws. Supporters of hate crime legislation argued that crimes motivated by prejudice against a social group were more serious and required stronger penalties as they threatened the security of not only the victim, but an entire group. In the following essay law professor James Jacobs argues that despite good intentions hate crime laws actually exacerbate racial tensions and are unlikely to have a deterrent effect.

On the one hand, to denounce hate crimes is to affirm the goal of a fair and tolerant society. On the other, to highlight the prejudicial and racial aspects of as many crimes as possible, transforming the crime problem into a prejudice problem, is to present an unduly bleak picture of the state of inter-group relations and rub salt into the wounds of festering angers and prejudices. Rather than defining violence as a social problem that unites all Americans in a search for a solution, this new approach defines the problem as a composite of different types of intergroup hate, and so may divide the political community.

Hate Crime Politics

In the last several years [during the early 1990s], New York City has experienced a new kind of political controversy: whether a particular crime merits denunciation as a hate crime by the criminal justice system, mayor, police commissioner, and media. These high visibility controversies put the politicians and police brass in a no-win situation. If they do not utter the words "hate crime," they are excoriated by the victim's group for bias and insensitivity. If they do apply the hate crime label, they are similarly criticized by the perpetrator's group for bias, hasty judgment, and double standards.

When the [April 1989] gang rape of the Central Park jogger was not classified as a hate crime (because a few of the victims of the marauding youths were black or Hispanic), some journalists charged that there exists a double standard, whereby white-on-black crimes are labeled hate crimes, while black-on-white crimes are not. Some women expressed outrage that a gang rape was not considered a hate crime regardless of the racial element. Meanwhile, some black observers denounced the prosecution of the youths as itself racist. To take another example, after [New York] Mayor [David] Dinkins forcefully denounced the [December 1992] beating of Ralph Nimmons, a homeless black man, as a bias crime, the Jewish Lubavitcher community reacted angrily to the hate crime charge, claiming that Nimmons had been apprehended burglarizing a school.

The very existence of the hate crime label raises the political and social stakes in intergroup crimes. Groups are beginning to keep score cards. Applying or failing to apply the hate crime label triggers heated political battles. The result is not greater racial and ethnic harmony, but exacerbated social conflict. . . .

The Politics of Victimization

Hate crime legislation attempts . . . to import the civil rights paradigm into criminal law. Some groups are defined as needing special protection against discriminatory treatment, albeit not at the hands of government officials or employers, but at the hands of criminals.

If such a status is available, every conceivable minority group will naturally lobby to be included. If the law says that criminal conduct motivated by racism warrants enhanced punishment, why shouldn't crime conduct motivated by sexism and homophobia also be covered? Not surprisingly, many women cannot understand why rape and spouse abuse do not qualify as hate crimes motivated by gender prejudice. Gays and lesbians, who in other contexts have not been fully successful in obtaining recognition as a bona fide minority group entitled to social, legal, and economic advantages, have argued with incontrovertible logic that to ignore the history of gay-bashing in the formulation of hate crime legislation would itself constitute an act of blatant prejudice.

Women and gays and lesbians are slowly obtaining inclusion in hate crime statutes, although their inclusion is by no means universal or uncontroversial. In the state of New York, for example, the legislature has refused to pass a hate crime law that includes gays and lesbians. Some state legislators also have argued that the victimization of women is already recognized in specific criminal statutes. Perhaps without fully realizing it, legislators are resisting the temptation to expand the hate crime label to the extent that it becomes nearly co-extensive with crime itself.

But some states, like Wisconsin, include prejudice based upon mental or physical disability in their hate crime statues. Many other prejudices will undoubtedly be recognized over time (age, marital status, political memberships and beliefs). To exclude any group, once it petitions to have its victimization recognized as equivalent to that of other groups, would provoke justifiable anger. Except where a particular prejudice enjoys substantial support (e.g. anti-gay sentiment in some states), politicians will almost certainly bestow hate crime victim status on practically any group that can make its voice heard; there is no political payoff in opposing such a demand. Eventually, a large percentage of all crimes could qualify for secondary condemnation as hate crimes. At that point, those whose victimizations do not fall within any hate crime category might feel discriminated against.

Hate crime law fits uneasily within the civil rights paradigm. Civil rights laws attempt to extend positive rights and opportunities to minorities and women. They are directed at the conduct of government officials and private persons who govern, regulate, or sell goods and services. By contrast, hate crime law deals with conduct that is already criminal and with wrongdoers who are already criminals. The possibility that criminals can be threatened into not discriminating in their choice of crime victims seems slight. Whether the criminal law can be employed successfully in eradicating or reforming deep-rooted prejudices is doubtful.

Enchancing Deterrence

The horrendous crimes that provide the imagery and emotion for the passage of hate crime legislation are already so heavily punished under American law that any talk of "sentence enhancement" must be primarily symbolic. In fact, we have all the criminal and sentencing law we need to respond severely and punitively to criminal conduct inspired, in whole or in part, by prejudice.

I do not mean to say that the availability of enhanced punishments for hate crimes can never have any practical implications. When new powers are given to police and prosecutors, they will be used and from time to time make a difference. This is more likely to happen in low-level crimes which, because of overloaded dockets and jails, would otherwise fall through the cracks but for the added emphasis that a hate crime label might provide.

In speculating about the possible deterrent effect of hate crime laws, we need also take into account some facts about the offenders who commit these crimes. According to data from New York City and Los Angeles, the majority are teenagers. In New York City in 1990, over 50 percent of hate crime arrestees were under the age of nineteen, and over 20 percent were under sixteen. Ironically, hate crime laws do not apply to juveniles who are charged with "delinquency" rather than with specific code offenses. Moreover, when juveniles are convicted they are "committed" to juvenile institutions for indefinite terms, not "sentenced"; thus, sentencing enhancement statutes are not applicable. Even if they were, the youthful offenders who are arrested for such crimes are often alienated, impulsive, and generally hostile, hardly the kind of individuals likely to be deterred by sentencing enhancements.

Questioning Prejudice

Even if the new wave of hate crime laws does not deter any hate crimes, some advocates, believe these laws are justified because hate crimes are "worse" than other crimes in the same generic offense category and so deserve greater punishment. I agree that certain extremely violent, racist crimes warrant the most intense condemnation, but I would not be prepared to say that these crimes are without moral equals. Is it invariably worse to be raped by someone who hates you because of your race, rather than for your gender, appearance, social class, or for no reason at all? Is a racially bigoted rapist deserving of more condemnation than a "merely" hostile and anti-social rapist? Does it really matter whether the rapists in the Central Park jogger case were motivated in whole or in part by racism?

The most horrible crimes—murder, rape, kidnapping, arson—are so devastating that it seems to deprecate the victim's pain and anguish to conclude, as the hate crime laws do, that there is more trauma if the perpetrator is a bigot as well as a brute. If distinctions must be made, wouldn't a more neutral statute make more sense; i.e. a rape warrants enhanced punishment if it involves terror, torture, or substantial gratuitous violence beyond the rape itself? Sentencing law already provides this option in many states.

Those who lobby for more hate crime laws claim that a crime motivated by prejudice ought to be punished more severely than other crimes because the effects ripple out beyond the individual victim; all members of the victim's group are made less secure and, depending upon which groups are involved, there may be retaliation or group conflict. Once again, I believe that this conclusion is applicable to some hate crimes, but I do not believe that every hate crime (e.g. an act of shoving on the subway) generates serious social instability. Moreover, all sorts of crimes have serious social repercussions: carjackings, shootings and stabbings in schools and housing projects, "wildings" in parks, shootouts by rival gangs and drug dealers, and murderous attacks in subways. Over the last several decades, fear of crime has been a prime reason that hundreds of thousands, perhaps millions, of people have moved from cities to suburbs or from one neighborhood to another. Thus, it is surely an exaggeration to say that hate crimes are unique in their impact on people beyond the immediate victims.

The Wrong Tool

While many civil rights advocates view the passage of hate crime laws as a step toward the reduction of hate crimes and prejudice generally, I am skeptical. To fragment criminal law into specialized laws recognizing a moral hierarchy of motives and offender/victim configurations will have little, if any, crime-control benefit, while carrying serious risks for race relations and social harmony. The attempt to extend the civil rights paradigm to crimes committed by one private party against another is well-meaning but misguided. Prejudice and hate will not be stamped out by enhancing criminal penalties, and considerable damage may result from enforcing these laws. The new hate crime laws both reflect and contribute to the politicization of the crime problem and the criminal justice process, especially around issues of race, and thereby exacerbate social divisions and social conflict.

Reducing prejudice and hate must be a high priority for American society, but more criminal law is the wrong tool. We should exhaust all other strategies of social education and institution-building before pinning our hopes on the criminal law, which has, at best, a very unimpressive record in ameliorating social problems.

The Roots of Hate
Crime Legislation

Brian Levin

In the following selection, Brian Levin, a civil rights attorney and a professor of criminal justice at California State University, traces the history of hate crime legislation. Levin argues that hate crime laws can be traced back to attempts to control the activities of the Ku Klux Klan and the culture of racist lynchings that existed in late-nineteenth-century America. Legislators attempted to respond to Klan violence through the creation of laws designed specifically to combat the Klan, setting the framework for contemporary hate crime legislation. By the mid-1900s the civil rights movement had made headway in the desegregation of American society, resulting in renewed violence from the Klan. Once again, legislators were forced to respond through the creation of new laws, thereby producing the 1968 hate crime statute, which prohibits interference with a variety of federally guaranteed rights based on race, color, religion or national origin. While there have been several attempts to extend the protection guaranteed by the statute by adding sexual orientation, gender, and disability to the list of protected characteristics, these have thus far failed to pass in Congress. The 1968 statue stands as the current federal law concerning hate crimes.

Criminal laws that punish discriminatory "hate crime" offenses relating to race, religion, ethnicity, sexual orientation, gender, and other status characteristics trace their roots back to the nation's founding. Unlike today, in early America, status distinctions in law, particularly racial ones, were intended to restrict the exercise of civil rights. Today's hate

Brian Levin, "From Slavery to Hate Crime Laws: The Emergence of Race and Status-Based Protection in American Criminal Law," *Journal of Social Issues*, vol. 58, no. 2, 2002, pp. 227–45. © 2002 The Society for the Psychological Study of Social Issues. Reproduced by permission of Blackwell Publishers.

crime laws are the refined modern progeny of an important class of remedial post–Civil War laws and constitutional amendments. Although the Supreme Court has vigorously upheld enhanced punishment for hate crimes over the last decade, it has also established restrictions on the government's authority to punish bigoted conduct and expression. This article examines, through an analysis of historic cases, laws, and constitutional changes, the legal evolution that culminated in the passage of modern hate crime laws.

Although some commentators concentrate on contemporary "identity politics" or "new social movements" as key elements in the development of hate crime statutes and jurisprudence, the underpinnings for this evolving area of the law are rooted in the legal foundations, history, and customs of the nation (Jacobs & Potter, 1998; Jenness & Broad, 1997). The recent emergence of a hate crime category on the legal landscape came about only after other foundational issues relating to free expression, federalism, and the role of status characteristics were addressed.

Hate crimes may be defined as those offenses committed because of the actual or perceived status characteristic of another, or alternatively, as crimes where the motive is the actual or perceived status characteristic of another—usually, but not necessarily, the crime's victim or target. Status characteristics are those material attributes common to identifiable classes of people that society recognizes through law, tradition, or custom. The seeds for recognizing and eventually protecting on the basis of status are found in a history that often, and conversely, used status as a pretext for unfair treatment and the deprivation of rights. Although one of the most commonly identified status characteristics is race, there are others as well. Status characteristics need not be immutable like race; they can be changeable, like religion or age. It should be noted here, although it is beyond the scope of this article, that civil antidiscrimination laws have also been crucial to validating the recognition of status by our legal system. This article will chronologically trace the legal treatment afforded to race (Levin, 1999).

Race: A Pretext for Harmful Mistreatment

The text of the Declaration of Independence leaves the impression that the notion of harmful status-based deprivations did not exist at America's founding: "We hold these truths to be self evident, that all men are created equal." Yet status-based violence and deprivations are as old as the nation itself. After independence, for instance, voting rights excluded the majority of white males not wealthy enough to meet financial requirements, women, most free Blacks, Native Americans, and slaves. Women were excluded from most occupations and were considered chattel of their husbands. Many Americans, including a large number of children, were deprived of educational opportunities, a living wage, health care, safe working environments, and sanitary housing conditions based on classs (Kluger, 1975).

Slavery, however, by virtue of the breadth of its brutality and the nature of its proponents' justifications, stands out as the most horrendous case of race-based discrimination. Slavery is important to a contemporary analysis of hate crime because the bigoted precepts that justified it still resonate in the stereotypes that contribute to acts of discriminatory violence. Although slavery preceded the Constitution, that document and the judicial interpretations of it strengthened and further legitimized slavery and the bigotry that justified it. However, from a legal standpoint race-based slavery and the effort to eradicate it and its harmful side effects are essential to the development of hate crime jurisprudence (Higginbotham, 1996).

Neither the word *race* nor the word *slavery* appeared in the Constitution when it was ratified in 1787. As judge and legal scholar A. Leon Higginbotham (1996, p. 68) explained:

"'The founding fathers' refusal to use the word 'slavery' in the Constitution of 1787 reveals that they did not want to acknowledge to the world the legitimization of slavery and their persistent legitimization of the precept of black inferiority." Yet a careful reading of the Constitution (see Article 1§§ 2 and 9) includes important sections that vigorously protected slave states and slaveholders. Various other sections of Article 1 provided significant, yet indirect, protections for slavery as well.

For most of post-Revolution white America, it was axiomatic that African Americans were inferior. The climate of the era was such that a variety of factors, including economics, law, philosophy, politics, and cultural practices, rationalized the inferiority myth that sustained harmful discriminatory treatment. Although the abolition movement later became a powerful political and social force, slavery found significant protection from the growing political firestorm in Southern and federal court decisions. Even progressive Southern courts refused to provide basic legal protections to slaves brutalized by violent masters, acts that depicted racially motivated hatred (Higginbotham, 1996). In *State v. Mann* (1829), North Carolina Supreme Court Justice Thomas Ruffin, acknowledging the decision's "harshness," nonetheless overturned the conviction of a slave master for shooting an escaping female slave in the back. Ruffin declared that the law imposed a duty irrespective of harm to slaves: "The power of the master must be absolute to render the submission of the slave absolute."

In antebellum America, slave owners, bounty hunters, and slave patrols found an even more potent ally in the U.S. Supreme Court, which stood firmly behind federal efforts to protect slavery despite social and political battles on the issue (*Abelman v. Booth*, 1859; *Prigg v. Pennsylvania*, 1842). However, Chief Justice Roger Taney's sweeping lead opinion in *Scott v. Sandford* (1857) did more than guarantee complete protection of slavery from congressional interference. Its harsh bigotry mirrored and promoted the prevailing social attitude of millions of American whites outside the orbit of the abolitionist movement. The facts of the case revolve around a slave couple, Dred and Hariet Scott, who traveled between free areas and slave states with their owners, who also hired them out to others. On April 6, 1846, the Scotts filed suit in a state circuit court in St. Louis on a claim of assault and false imprisonment for being held as slaves. The Scotts contended that their entry into "free" jurisdictions altered their status from slaves to emancipated persons (*Scott v. Sandford*, 1857).

In dismissing the Scotts' claim, the Court held that Blacks, owing to their inferior nature, were incapable of being citizens of the United States and thus not subject to the privileges and immunities of citizenship (*Scott v. Sanford*, 1857). The Court recognized the Fifth Amendment constitutional rights of masters not to be deprived of their property without due process, rather than the humanity of African Americans.

Higginbotham (1996, p. 65) observed that the Supreme Court made twenty-one references in the Scott decision to the inferiority of African Americans, including the following:

> They had for more than a century before been regarded as beings of an inferior order, and altogether unfit to associate with the white race either in social or political relations, and so far inferior that they had no rights which the white man was bound to respect, and that the negro might justly and lawfully be reduced to slavery for his benefit. He was bought and sold, and treated as an ordinary article of merchandise and traffic whenever a profit could be made by it.
>
> This opinion was at that time fixed and universal in the civilized portion of the white race. It was regarded as an axiom in morals as well as in politics which no one thought of disputing or supposed to be open to dispute, and men in every grade and position in society daily and habitually acted upon it in their private pursuits, as well as in matters

of public concern, without doubting for a moment the correctness of this opinion. (*Scott v. Sandford*, 1857, p. 407).

Even prominent politicians opposed to slavery made clear their racial prejudices to voters, lest opponents mischaracterize their positions. In his famous 1858 senatorial election debates with Stephen Douglas, Abraham Lincoln sounded much like an educated version of a modern-day white supremacist. He favored relocation in Africa for the "inferior" American Blacks. His complete opposition for legal and social parity for Blacks extended into the areas of suffrage, service in public office, jury service, and intermarriage. Lincoln further stated that "there is a physical difference between the races which I believe will forever forbid the two races living together on terms of social and political equality" (Blaustein and Zangrando, 1991, p. 171).

The increasingly violent Civil War forced Lincoln, as president, away from an initial gradualist approach to abolition. His January 1, 1863, Emancipation Proclamation "freed" only those slaves in areas in rebellion and did not apply to Northern border states. Lincoln used his emergency war power authority to free slaves, but that power could extend only to areas where it could be said military authority had jurisdiction (U.S. Constitution, Article II).

The war's aftermath left four million southern Blacks in a state of legal limbo. While in free Northern states Blacks constituted 4 percent or less of the population, in the various Confederate states Blacks were between 26 percent and 59 percent of the population (Foner & Garraty, 1991a). The following section analyzes the sociological tensions that influenced the status and treatment of free Blacks in the post–Civil War era and beyond.

Initial Application of Status-Based Protections

Two conflicting events in December 1865 would profoundly affect the status of African Americans in the South. The first was the ratification of the Thirteenth Amendment, which abolished slavery. The second was the founding of the Ku Klux Klan, the nation's largest and most enduring terrorist group. Founded initially as an informal fraternity by six educated Civil War veterans, the Klan soon developed into a wide-ranging rural terror group, particularly after it came under the leadership of former Confederate war general Nathan Bedford Forrest in 1867. The Klan's violent campaign of intimidation was waged against newly freed Blacks, and whites who supported Reconstruction (Chalmers, 1981). Under Forrest's leadership and for a short time thereafter, Klan violence, which included terrorist threats, assaults, and homicides, limited the application of the new social, legal, and political protections promised to African Americans (Higginbotham, 1996). New, sweeping Constitutional and statutory reforms cut off the traditional legal and political methods Whites relied on to deprive Blacks of their rights (Higginbotham, 1996). Although their initial success was fleeting, these new, egalitarian postwar reforms laid the foundation for changes that extended into the latter half of the next century, including the emergence of hate crime laws. They represented a newfound validation of federal authority in the area of criminal law and supremacy of national power over that of the states to protect minorities from the harms of race-based violence and discrimination (Chalmers, 1981; Higginbotham, 1996).

After the passage of the Thirteenth Amendment, the next action to protect newly freed slaves was the Civil Rights Act of 1866, a precursor to the Fourteenth Amendment, which attempted to secure citizenship for southern Blacks and provide them with equal protection under the laws. The statute provided for criminal penalties against government officials who deprived inhabitants of civil rights and all who aided in the obstruction of authorities in the enforcement of civil rights. It was in 1868, however, that the most monumental substantive change in civil rights materialized with the passage of the

Fourteenth Amendment, which overturned the holding of *Scott v. Sandford* by guaranteeing both state and national citizenship to newly freed slaves. Although the Civil Rights Act of 1866 also extended citizenship and other rights to Blacks, many contended that Congress lacked the authority to pass legislation of that sort, absent a constitutional amendment (Higginbotham, 1996).

The Fourteenth Amendment's coverage of Blacks and other Americans as state and national citizens was of great import. Previously, the Constitution's protections had extended only to deprivations by the federal government against citizens, leaving the states unrestricted authority to interfere with individual civil rights. The amendment's conferring of national citizenship now inoculated those who possessed it, at least in theory, with protection from state interference with civil rights as well (Higginbotham, 1996).

The Fifteenth Amendment, ratified in 1870, guaranteed that voting rights would not be limited on account of race, color, or previous condition of slavery. After racist violence was highlighted in congressional hearings, companion legislation was enacted that provided criminal penalties for those who interfere with voting rights. The 1871 Force Act also dealt with suffrage by providing enhanced federal authority to protect the franchise of African Americans. The Ku Klux Klan Act of 1871 criminally punished government officials and private conspiracies when they operated to deprive citizens of equal protection or interfered with federal protection of civil rights. The last piece of civil rights legislation for the next 75 years was the Civil Rights Act of 1875, which guaranteed "full and equal enjoyment to all citizens of public accomodations, places of public amusement, and conveyances regardless of their race, color, or previous condition of servitude." These three post–Civil War laws and amendments for the first time codified the government's obligation to combat status-based mistreatment and criminality, a key legal justification that extends to modern hate crime laws. Unfortunately, as the discussion in the next section shows, the prejudices of the day extended to the U.S. Supreme Court, which determined the range and potency of these newfound protections.

The Supreme Court's Assault on Status-Based Legal Protections

With few exceptions, the Supreme Court eviscerated the post–Civil War era statutory and constitutional protections in subsequent years (Higginbotham, 1996). The Court was influenced in doing so by the prejudices of most of its members and a judicial philosophy that was hostile to the expanding growth of federal authority over that of the states. In 1872, for example, in *Blyew v. United States*, the Court threw out the federal murder convictions of two White defendants convicted of hacking an innocent Black family to death in Kentucky; the murders were committed as a preemptive strike in a future race war. Kentucky state law at the time did not allow the statements of African American witnesses to be used against white defendants, so prosecutors, relying on the Civil Rights Act of 1866, tried the case in federal court, where the witnesses' statements would be allowed. The statute permitted federal courts to be used when crime victims and those immediately affected had been denied enforcement in state courts. The Supreme Court, in throwing out the conviction, held that it was the defendants who were affected by the enforcement, rather than the dead victims or the witnesses (i.e., that the law was not intended to give victims and witnesses the chance to testify [that is, in fact, what the law intended] but to protect the defendants; *Bylew v. United States*, 1872). The contorted reasoning of the decision sent a clear message that in the area of racial violence the Court would combat federal intervention whenever possible.

In 1876, the Court in *United States v. Reese* invalidated portions of the 1870 Enforcement Act that punished state officials who interfered with Black voting rights, stating that the federal government lacked the authority to pass the legislation. In a companion case the Court threw out the indictments of three white Louisianans convicted of using violence to stop Blacks from voting. The case arose from the Easter 1873 massacre of scores of Blacks by armed former Klansmen who had attempted to secure a local courthouse on behalf of a Republican gubernatorial candidate in a disputed election. As a result of arguably the worst single act of Reconstruction-era racial violence, ninety-seven indictments were issued under the 1870 Enforcement Act. Only three defendants were ultimately convicted, and those only on conspiracy charges (Higginbotham, 1996, p. 88; *United States v. Reese*, 1876).

Neither the Supreme Court nor the majority of the white American public was ready for the exercise of equality that many Reconstruction-era laws promised. By the time the Supreme Court invalidated the Civil Rights Act of 1875 in 1883, Blacks had been subjected to severe economic deprivation, racially motivated violence, and unequal segregation (*Civil Rights Cases*, 1883). Most judicial opinions relating to other status groups, including women and immigrants, were similarly restrictive.

The fact of the matter is that the law and judicial decisions of the times reflected the prevailing supremacist social and political attitudes of much of the white American populace. These attitudes in turn led to a new wave of hatred and violence that continued into the next century. The continued violence prompted new atempts to curtail not only the brutality, but also the groups and messages that promoted it (Higginbotham, 1996).

The Next Wave: Lynchings, Klan Rebirth, and Early Antihate Laws

The demise of the organized Klan in the 1870s led to a new type of spontaneous racial terrorism: lynching. Lynchings are those crimes in which violent mobs fatally attack someone who is thought to have violated the law or social mores of a particular locality. American lynchings were generally exercises in public mob torture where victims were mutilated, burned, or hung until they died. Before being coopted by racists, lynching had previously emerged as a punishment of choice by frontier vigilantes from the Revolutionary era into the late 1800s. Thereafter there were a variety of targets and motives for lynchings, but most were directed against African Americans. Of the 4,743 Americans known to have been lynched, 3,446 were Black (Foner & Garraty, 1991b).

Although sixteen states passed antilynching laws between the 1890s and the 1930s, the laws were rarely enforced in a meaningful way. The National Association for the Advancement of Colored People, beginning in 1918, proposed national legislation as a way to give federal courts jurisdiction over lynching crimes. It was hoped that federal prosecutions would bring perpetrators to justice in cases in which local officials were either complicit with or sympathetic to the killers. Congressional bills passed the House of Representatives in 1922, 1937, and 1940 but failed to become law owing to Senate opposition (Foner & Garraty, 1991b).

In addition to individual lynchings, race riots directed against Blacks also gained notoriety, with twenty-three taking place just in the decade from 1910 to 1920. One race riot alone in East Saint Louis, Illinois, left forty-seven people dead ("Race Riots," 1975). In the aftermath of violent rioting, Illinois became the first state to pass a "group-libel" statute, which punished those who made bigoted "defamatory" statements against racial, religious, or ethnic groups. No federal group-libel statute was ever passed, and such statutes were rarely used in those states that enacted them (Walker, 1994). Although the Supreme Court upheld Illinois's group-libel statute in 1952, most legal scholars today contend that the decision is invalid because it conflicts with subsequent holdings (*Beauharnais v. Illinois*, 1952; *R.A.V. v. St. Paul*, 1992; Walker, 1994).

The rebirth of the second-era Ku Klux Klan in 1915–1925 also had an influence on hate violence and legislation. When the Klan's second era commenced in 1915 the scope of Klan bigotry expanded to include new enemies in addition to African Americans: Catholics, Jews, and new immigrants. Klan ideology embraced the trappings of Protestant fundamentalism, extreme patriotism, social conservatism, and xenophobia. By the mid 1920s, the Klan had 4.5 million members throughout the East and Northwest, with a disproportionate representation in Indiana. (Indiana and other heartland states had a significant Klan representation because of an aggressive Klan strategy to recruit rural conservative Protestants both inside and outside the South.) Across the nation Klan members held positions as governors, state legislators, and congressmen. During this same period rampant Klan violence was publicized in congressional hearings and intensive newspaper coverage (Bullard, 1991; Chalmers, 1981; Ridgeway, 1995).

As a response to Klan violence various jurisdictions passed laws designed to specifically combat the Klan. Antimasking laws, which prohibited the nontheatrical wearing of masks in public, were passed in various states. Municipal authorities with substantial Catholic populations from New England to the Great Lakes region confiscated Klan materials or banned the group from meeting or parading (Walker, 1994). In 1923 New York enacted a sweeping anti-Klan statute that compelled various "oath-bound" groups deemed illegitimate by the state to register with authorities and disclose their membership. The statute also banned the wearing of masks in public. In 1928 the Supreme Court upheld New York's restrictions on governmentally disfavored organizations, like the Klan, on the grounds that it was proper to do so as a legitimate exercise of state authority (*Bryant v. Zimmerman*, 1928). Antilynching, group-libel, and anti-Klan laws had limited impact at the time, but they provided further foundation for the concept that the criminal law should be used to combat various manifestations of bigotry, a key development that led to the more refined hate crime laws of today.

Third-Era Klan Violence Brings More Statutory Changes

Hate violence in the South received renewed national attention during the civil rights era. As was the case previously, white supremacists, and the Klan in particular, reacted violently when legal and political developments ran counter to their goals. The walls of societal segregation, reinforced by the legal decision in *Plessy v. Ferguson* [the landmark decision that approved racial segregation in public facilities] five decades earlier, began to crumble in the late 1940s with the integration of baseball and the military and the Supreme Court's rejection of racially restrictive housing deeds. By 1954, the Supreme Court for the first time invalidated the doctrine of separate but equal, first upheld by the Court in *Plessy (Brown v. Board of Education*, 1954). Although technically *Brown* applied only to the area of public education, it was clear to integrationists and segregationists alike that constitutional protection for segregation in public life had come to an end and that it was only a matter of time before other cases applied the integrationist holding of *Brown* to other contexts.

Other branches of government also set the tone against racial discrimination. President [Dwight D.] Eisenhower [1953–1961], [Lyndon B.] Johnson [1963–1969], and [John F.] Kennedy [1961–1963] all promoted civil rights legislation and took public positions against Southern intransigence. Constitutional amendments and various pieces of federal civil, voting, and housing rights legislation were enacted between 1957 and 1968. Thus, the third-era Klan of the early 1960s had a significant sociopolitical goal in fighting desegregation efforts through intimidation and violence. By 1964 one of the most violent Klan groups, the Mississippi White Knights, undertook a series of carefully planned attacks to retaliate against activists involved in Freedom Summer educational and voting initiatives. In a preemptive April strike, scores of crosses were burned across the state in one night. On May 3, 1964, the group's imperial wizard, Sam Bowers, issued an executive order to his membership to engage in "counterattacks" against "selected individual targets." During the summer there were eighty racially motivated assaults, including thirty-five shootings, twenty church arsons, and five murders (Bullard, 1993; Chalmers, 1981).

Much of the Mississippi hate violence and all five murders were at the hands of White Knight members. Three of those murdered were civil rights workers James Chaney, a Black native Mississippian, and white Northerners Andrew Goodman and Michael Schwerner, who were killed by Klansmen with the assistance of Neshoba County Deputy Sheriff Cecil Price (Bullard, 1993). Less than one month later three unarmed Black Army reservists were attacked by a self-described Klan "security force" on a highway near Athens, Georgia. Lt. Col. Lemuel Penn, an education administrator from Washington, D.C., was killed by a shotgun blast to the neck. The following summer Viola Liuzzo, a white mother of five, was shot to death by Klansmen in Lowndes County, Alabama, as she drove a Black civil rights worker from Selma to Montgomery (Bullard, 1993; Chalmers, 1981). Various defendants in the Neshoba, Mississippi, murders and the Penn case appealed the use of federal criminal civil rights laws in their prosecution as far as the Supreme Court, where they lost (*United States v. Guest*, 1966; *United States v. Price*, 1966). The national media coverage given to Klan violence and police brutality against innocent African Americans decisively turned the social and political leanings of the nation toward heightened civil rights enforcement and legislative reform.

New Laws to Combat Hate Violence in the Post-Civil Rights Era

Currently, the most widely used federal criminal civil rights law applicable to hate crime is 18 U.S.C. 245, "Federally Protected Rights." This statute, enacted in 1968, was Congress's response to Klan violence in the South during the civil rights era. ("U.S.C." refers to the United States Code, where all federal legislation can be found. The number on the left refers to the volume number, and the number on the right is the section number.) Congressional action was fueled by extensive hearings on Klan violence in 1965 and the unequivocal Supreme Court approval of 18 U.S.C. 241 and 242 the following year in the cases arising out of the murders of Schwerner, Goodman, Chaney, and Penn (*United States v. Guest*, 1966; *United States v. Price*, 1966). The 1968 statute prohibits interference with voting, obtaining government or federally funded benefits or services, accessing federal employment, or participation in a federal jury. Among other things the law also punishes the interference with six other federally protected activities, but only when such interference is committed on the basis of race, color, religion, or national origin. These protected activities include enrollment in public education, participation in state programs, obtaining private or state employment, participation in state and local jury service, interstate travel, and the benefits of various types of public accommodations.

In 1998, 1999, and 2000 Congress failed to pass bills that would amend 18 U.S.C. 245 by adding sexual orientation, gender, and disability to the protected characteristics and by broadly expanding the protected rights beyond the narrow list enumerated over thirty years ago (Hate Crime Prevention Act of 1999). The addition of these new group categories remains controversial, because protection on the basis of race and religion has a long constitutional precedent that extends back to the First Amendment in 1791 and the post–Civil War Amendments, whereas these newer categories lack such a history. Newer proposed status characteristics such as sexual orientation were included in legislative proposals in part because of an expansive political mobilization by coordinated segments of the gay and lesbian community—a new and somewhat controversial factor (Jeness & Broad, 1997). Hate crime laws refer to newer pieces of legislation that protect a wide range of status characteristics from a broad array of crimes. In contrast criminal civil rights laws are structured to resemble the post–Civil War legal protections, which primarily invoked race, and later other status characteristics, as a dependent factor to the primary protection of various enumerated rights, such as voting or use of a public accommodation (Higginbotham, 1996; Levin, 1999).

Today, hate crime laws actually reflect a broad category of offenses that cover prohibitions against cross burnings and desecration to houses of worship and cemeteries, as well as antimasking laws, penalty enhancements, and stand-alone civil rights or intimidation statutes. It is these last two types of statutes, the penalty enhancements and the stand-alone statutes, that are the most broadly applicable to the widest range of criminal conduct, and these are the ones that are most commonly referred to as "hate crime" statutes. Notwithstanding the protests of critics, hate crime laws are consistent with the traditional aims of criminal law. Criminal law in general, and hate crime laws in particular, adjust punishment among instances of seemingly similar conduct according to the type of victim, the context of the offense, the offender's motive, the severity of the result, and the effect on the overall community (Levin, 1999).

State and Local Hate Crime Initiatives

Renewed awareness about hate crime influenced public policy starting in the late 1970s. Boston launched the first police unit in the United States aimed at combating discriminatory crime in 1978 after civil strife erupted over court-ordered busing. In 1979 Massachusetts enacted the first modern law aimed at hate crime with the passage of a civil rights statute—the Massachusetts Civil Rights Act—that protects civil rights without regard to status characteristics (Levin, 1992–1993; Mass. Ann. Laws chap. 265, § 37). Although the Massachusetts law omits mention of status groups, authorities made it clear through aggressive enforcement that it covered racial and religious-based "hate crimes." In 1981 the Anti-Defamation League (ADL) drafted model legislation to combat institutional vandalism against houses of worship, cemeteries, and public institutions. It also drafted a model penalty enhancement statute, based in part on federal law that increased penalties for those who commit crimes because of the victims' actual or perceived race, religion, or national origin. The ADL's model was amended to include sexual orientation later in the decade and gender in 1995 (ADL, 1991; Rosenberg & Lieberman, 1999). By 1985 Rhode Island, Connecticut, New York, Illinois, Pennsylvania, Oregon, and Washington State had broad criminal laws that punished those who committed crimes on the basis of race, national origin/ethnicity, and religion. Rhode Island had an additional law that protected legal immigrants, and Washington State covered disability (National Institute Against Prejudice and Violence, 1986).

Starting in 1979 new private monitoring organizations such as the National Anti-Klan Network and the Southern Poverty Law Center's Klanwatch focused national attention on a resurgence of harms associated with violence by hate groups. In 1979 the ADL published its first comprehensive national audit of anti-Semitic incidents. In 1983 the U.S. Commission on Civil Rights issued a report urging further examination of bias-motivated violence. The issue of hate violence gained momentum as consortiums developed among law enforcement, civil rights groups, victims' rights organizations, and religious, gay, ethnic and other advocacy groups (Levin, 1999).

This increased attention resulted in more serious treatment of misdemeanors and other crimes that would have otherwise garnered minimal sanctions. States such as California also enacted hate crime laws that increased the penalty for repeat hate crime offenders or those who commit hate crimes in groups. Other laws also allow victims of hate violence to obtain civil injunctions and monetary damages (California Penal Code §§ 422.6, 422.75; California Civil Code § 52). By 1991, twenty-nine states had hate crime laws, with the number increasing to forty-one by 2000 (Levin, 1999; National Institute Against Prejudice and Violence, 1988).

Modern Federal Hate Crime Measures and Reporting

During the 1990s four new pieces of hate crime legislation were introduced at the federal level. The first was the Hate Crime Statistics Act, signed into law by President George H.W. Bush [1989–1993] in April 1990. The act initially required the attorney general to collect data on crimes motivated by race, religion, sexual orientation, and ethnicity and was subsequently amended to include disability. In 2000 an admitted undercount of 8,063 hate crime incidents was reported. Out of 16,000 law enforcement agencies in the United States 11,690 "participated" in the data collection program administered under the Act in 1999, but only 16.2 percent reported incidents in 2000 within their jurisdiction.

In 1994 the Hate Crime Sentencing Enhancement Act was enacted. The statute, a penalty enhancement law, increases the sentence for underlying federal offenses by about 30 percent when the fact finder establishes beyond a reasonable doubt that the target is intentionally selected because of race, color, religion, national origin, ethnicity, gender, disability, or sexual orientation. The law's practical limitation is that it is applicable only to a relatively small number of substantive underlying federal offenses. In 1996, after a series of well-publicized church arsons around the country, Congress enacted new legislation broadening coverage and increasing the penalties for such crimes.

Initially introduced in 1998, the Hate Crime Prevention Act has failed to come to a vote in the House of Representatives despite affirmative votes in the Senate as late as June 2000. Support for the bill intensified after a string of nationally publicized hate murders that included the dragging murder of James Byrd in Jasper, Texas, and the homophobic beating of Wyoming college student Matthew Shepard. The bill would alter the main federal criminal civil rights statute, 18 U.S.C. 245, in two significant ways. First, it would extend federal legal protection on the basis of gender, disability, and sexual orientation, but only in cases involving interstate commerce. The other statutory reform the bill would provide is a broadening of the circumstances protected. Currently, 18 U.S.C. 245 requires that prosecutors establish that a particular victim was attacked both because of his status and because of his exercise of a particular protected activity listed in the statute.

Some commentators mistakenly assert the unconstitutionality of hate crime laws because these laws mention status characteristics. However, hate crime laws, like their civil law antidiscrimination counterparts, are constitutional because they apply equally to all members of the status groups that they cover. Thus, hate crime laws that punish racial attacks are valid because they punish all racially based attacks, not merely those against a particular racial group. The fact that a particular law covers only some status characteristics, but not others, is also an insufficient basis to invalidate the statute on Fourteenth Amendment grounds (*Railway Express Agency v. New York*, 1949).

The Supreme Court Establishes Limits on Punishing Hateful Offenders

In two modern cases the Supreme Court has set rules relating to when a person's hateful beliefs can be used in death penalty cases in *Barclay v. Florida* (1983), the Court upheld the death sentence of a Black defendant given by a judge who relied on the defendant's racial motivation for the murder. In *Dawson v. Delaware* (1992), the court overturned a death sentence that was imposed in part on the basis of a convict's membership in a white supremacist group in a murder case in which his racist beliefs and associations were not relevant to the crime. The Court found that a defendant's abstract beliefs were an impermissible basis on which to impose criminal punishment.

In the 1992 case of *R.A.V. v. St. Paul*, the Court ruled on the constitutionality of a 1989 municipal "hate speech" ordinance used to prosecute a teenage skinhead for burning a cross in the yard of an African American family. In its first ruling on the topic since 1952, the Court unanimously invalidated the statute, although the justices were deeply divided as to why. All nine justices agreed that the ordinance was impermissibly overbroad in its restrictions by punishing speech that merely evoked anger or resentment. The Court has consistently construed the First Amendment over recent decades as protecting extremely offensive speech and political discourse that fails to rise to the level of a threat, immediate inticement to criminality, or solicitation of a crime. The offensiveness of an idea is an impermissible basis for the government to punish expression (*Texas v. Johnson*, 1989). Four of the justices in *R.A.V. v. St. Paul* supported the position that it was constitutional to punish expression whose severity went beyond merely offending someone. Since threats and so-called fighting words were traditionally held to be unprotected by the First Amendment, these justices maintained that it was permissible for the government to selectively punish bigoted speeh within these categories on the basis of the idea expressed. In a dissenting opinion that foreshadowed the Court's next hate crime ruling, Associate Justice John Paul Stevens contended:

> Conduct that creates special risks or harms may be prohibited by special rules. Lighting a fire near an ammunition dump or a gasoline storage tank is especially dangerous;

such behavior may be punished more severely than burning trash in a vacant lot. Threatening someone because of her race or religious beliefs may cause particularly severe trauma or touch off a riot . . . such conduct may be punished more severely than threats against someone based on, way, his support of a particular athletic team. (*R.A.V. v. St. Paul*, p. 416)

The controlling opinion, authored by Associate Justice Antonin Scalia, held differently. The five prevailing justices expressed their belief that even traditionally "unprotected" areas of speech are afforded a baseline of protection that prevents the government from further subdivision in order to punish some viewpoints, but not others, within that "unprotected" category. They held that punishing certain types of threatening cross burnings, such as those based on racial supremacy, but not others, such as those degrading the mentally ill, violated that principle. The *R.A.V.* decision invalidated those hate crime laws in which the criminality of a particular act hinged solely on the idea expressed through the use of a particular symbol. The ruling had the additional effect of invalidating speech codes at public universities throughout the United States. In 1996, the Court, without comment, refused to grant review of a challenge to a Florida law that criminalized all hostile cross burning on the property of another. That law, unlike St. Paul's ordinance, did not differentiate cross burnings on the basis of the hateful idea expressed (*State v. T.B.D.*, 1995, 1996).

Wisconsin v. Mitchell: The Court Affirms Hate Crime Laws

The issue of the overall validity of hate crime laws as a category was settled in 1993 in *Wisconsin v. Mitchell*, in which the Court unanimously upheld the constitutionality of another type of hate crime statute: penalty enhancement laws. The specific enhancement law at issue in *Wisconsin v. Mitchell* punished an offender's intentional selection of a victim or property based on the victim's status characteristics, including race, religion, color, national origin, and ancestry. Todd Mitchell was a 19-year-old African American resident of Kenosha, Wisconsin, angered over a scene in the movie *Mississippi Burning*, where an African American child was beaten by white supremacists as he knelt to pray. Mitchell incited a crowd to viciously beat Gregory Riddick, a white 14-year-old passerby. Mitchell was convicted of aggravated battery—party to a crime and sentenced to two years for the underlying assault. He was sentenced to another two-year term for intentionally selecting his victim on account of race, for a total of four years' incarceration out of a potential maximum seven-year term (Levin, 1999; *Wisconsin v. Mitchell*, 1993).

In reversing the Wisconsin Supreme Court, the U.S. Supreme Court, in an opinion by Chief Justice William Rehnquist, cited three basic reasons for affirming the statute. First, the Court noted that although the government may not punish abstract beliefs, it can punish a vast array of depraved motives. Second, the Court further found that penalty enhancement laws, unlike the statute at issue in *R.A.V. v. St. Paul*, did not prevent people from expressing their views or punish them for doing so. Lastly, the Court pointed to the severity of hate crimes' harms, stating that they are "thought to be more likely to provoke retaliatory crimes, inflict distinct emotional harm on their victims and incite community unrest."

Although a vast consortium, ranging from police fraternal organizations to the American Civil Liberties Union, filed briefs supporting the decision, not everyone was pleased with the outcome. Some prominent legal scholars contended that punishing discriminatory crimes more severely than other crimes was merely a subtly disguised legalistic end run to punish disfavored thoughts. New York University Law Professor James Jacobs and attorney Kimberly Potter (1998) criticized the Mitchell decision as follows: "The very facts of that case present a defendant who is punished more severely, based on viewpoints" (p. 129). Conservative commentator George Will (1998) referred to hate crime laws as "moral pork barrel" and an "imprudent extension of identity politics."

After the *Mitchell* decision, Wisconsin's intentional selection model, presumably because of its affirmation by the Court, became the preferred model for new hate crime legislation (see, e.g., Hate Crime Sentencing Enhancement Act of 1994). Although hate speech laws have been roundly rejected in the United States, that is not the case in most of the Western world, as the next section illustrates (Walker, 1994).

In Canada, the Sentencing Reform Bill (C-41) is a penalty enhancement provision, similar to those in the United States, that allows for increased sentences when a crime is committed because of someone's nationality, color, religion, sex, age, mental or physical disability, or sexual orientation. In addition, Canada has far more expansive hate speech laws that are common to other Western nations with less stringent protections of free speech. Section 318 of the Canadian Criminal Code criminally punishes those who "advocate genocide" on the basis of color, race, religion, or ethnic origin. Section 319(1) punishes those who incite hatred on the basis of "color, race, religion, or ethnic origin where such incitement is likely to lead to a breach of the peace." Section 319(2) punishes the public communication of statements that willfully promote hatred on the basis of color, race, religion, or ethnic origin.

In the United Kingdom the primary laws that punish racial hatred are located in Part III of the Public Order Act of 1986 ((1) §§ 17 et seq.) and Part II of the Crime and Disorder Act of 1998. The statutes punish the incitement of racial hatred through words, conduct, or the display of written material. The laws expansively define race as including color, race, nationality (including citizenship), and ethnic or national origins. Germany also has a criminal law that punishes inciting racial hatred. In 1996 American Gerhard Lauck was sentenced to four years in prison by a German court after authorities apprehended him during a European trip. Lauck was convicted for the mass mailing of hateful neo-Nazi materials to Germany, where it is banned, from his home in Nebraska, where it is legal. Article 5 of the German Constitution provides limited protection for free speech, but only to the extent that the expression is truthful and does not contravene the human rights of others (Rosenberg and Kessler, 2000).

Conclusion: Public Policy Issues

The concept of protecting individuals from status-based violence began with legal attempts to eradicate the harmful effects of racially based slavery in the immediate post–Civil War period. Subsequent reforms would be proposed in the wake of public outrage over lynchings, race riots, Klan terrorism, and contemporary hate crimes. These proposed reforms were not always immediately sustained, because they were often limited by a change in public opinion, political opposition, or judicial rebuke. Nevertheless, profound cumulative changes took place over time that altered the social, legal, and political landscape of the nation. As committed journalists, scholars, activists, and lawyers exposed the harms of violent bigotry, public sentiment, political will, and judicial temperment changed to a point at which criminal law, particularly federal criminal law, was altered. Federal law changed from being a tool of minority oppression to one of minority protection. Still, the courts and politics have placed limits on the extent of the protection offered by federal law. Although the modern Supreme Court has affirmed the constitutionality of hate crime laws, it has also set limits relating to hate speech and federal jurisdictional issues (Levin, 1999).

As a result of the post–Civil War amendments to the Constitution, the federal government has wider jurisdictional latitude to protect on the basis of race and ethnicity. State legislatures, which already have primary jurisdiction over criminal legislation, are free to pass hate crime laws and include whatever status characteristics they see fit, without the limitations that face federal lawmakers. Forty-two states now have broadly applicable laws that cover at least race, religion, and national origin. There will be political debate in the eight states without hate crime laws regarding the enactment of new laws, and in those states that do not cover certain categories like gender and sexual orientation about the amendment of their laws.

The Internet will present important legal issues with respect to hate crimes. Domestically, local jurisdictions and the federal government will have to coordinate their efforts to apprehend people, like white supremacists, who use the Internet to threaten people or cause punishable harms in other jurisdictions. Moreover, internationally, choice-of-law conflicts exist between the United States and those countries whose criminal laws punish hate speech, something U.S. law does not do. The United States does not generally extradite to other nations for offenses that are not crimes here. However, foreign nations that criminalize hate speech will face the difficult task of asserting physical custody over individuals in the United States who commit offenses in their countries via the Internet without actually being physically present there.

As the harms of hate crimes have been exposed, that exposure has enabled advocacy groups to set in motion a series of criminal law reforms that legislatures, the courts, and the public have generally supported. However, the public policy debate has not always resulted in immediate reform or even agreement as to the extent and nature of these reforms. One thing is sure: Hate crime laws are now a permanent part of the American legal landscape, even as debate continues as to who should be protected by these laws, when they should be triggered, and which authorities should be able to enforce them.

References

1. Abelman v. Booth, 21 How. 506 (1859).

2. Anti-Defamation League (ADL). *Hate crime statutes: A 1991 status report*. New York: Author.
3. Barclay v. Florida, 463 U.S. 939 (1983).
4. Beauharnais v. Illinois, 343 U.S. 250 (1952).
5. Blaustein, A., and Zangrando, R. (Eds.). (1991). *Civil rights and African Americans*. Evanston, IL: Northwestern University Press.
6. Blyew v. United States, 80 U.S. 581 (1872).
7. Brandenburg v. Ohio, 395 U.S. 444 (1969).
8. Broad, K., and Jenness, V. (1997). *New social movements and the politics of violence*. New York: Aldine de Gruyter.
9. Brown v. Board of Education, 347 U.S. 483 (1954).
10. Bryant v. Zimmerman, 278 U.S. 63 (1928).
11. Bullard, S. (Ed.). (1991). *Special Report: The Ku Klux Klan: A History of Racism and Violence* (4th ed.). Montgomery, AL: Southern Poverty Law Center.
12. Bullard, S. (Ed.). (1993). *Free at Last: A History of the Civil Rights Movement and those who Died in the Struggle*. Montgomery, AL: Southern Poverty Law Center.
13. Chalmers, D.M. (1981). *Hooded Americanism*. New York: Franklin Watts.
14. Civil Rights Cases, 109 U.S. 3 (1883).
15. Dawson v. Delaware, 503 U.S. 159 (1992).
16. Federal Bureau of Investigation. (2000). *Hate Crimes in the United States: 1999*. Washington, DC: U.S. Department of Justice.
17. Foner, E., and Garraty, J. (Eds.). (1991a). Civil War. In *The Reader's Companion to American History* (p. 185). Boston: Houghton Mifflin.
18. Foner, E., and Garraty, J. (Eds.). (1991b). Lynching. In *The Reader's Companion to American History* (pp. 685–686). Boston: Houghton Mifflin.
19. Hate Crime Prevention Act, S. 622, 106th Cong. (1999).
20. Hate Crime Sentencing Enhancement Act. Violent Crime Control and Law Enforcement Act, § 280003 (Public Law 103–322), 108 Stat. 1796, 2096 (1994).
21. Hate Crime Statistics Act, 28 U.S.C. 534 (1990).
22. Higginbotham, A.L. (1996). *Shades of Freedom*. Oxford University Press: New York.
23. Jacobs, J., and K. Potter (1998). *Hate Crimes: Criminal Law and Identity Politics*. New York: Oxford University Press.
24. Jenness, V., and K. Broad (1997). *Hate Crimes: New Social Movements and the Politics of Violence*. Hawthorne, NY: Aldine de Gruyter.
25. Kluger, R. (1975). *Simple Justice*. New York: Random House.
26. Ku Klux Klan Act, 18 U.S.C. 241 (1871).
27. Levin, B. (1992–1993). Bias Crimes: A Theoretical and Practical Overview. *Stanford Law & Policy Review, 4*, 165–180.
28. Levin, B. (1999). Hate Crime: Worse by Definition. *Journal of Contemporary Criminal Justice, 15*, 6–21.
29. Mass. Ann. Laws, chap 265 § 37.
30. National Institute Against Prejudice and Violence. (1986). *Striking Back at Bigotry*. Baltimore, MD: Author.
31. National Institute Against Prejudice and Violence. (1988). *Striking Back at Bigotry*. Supplement. Baltimore, MD: Author.
32. Plessy v. Ferguson, 163 U.S. 537 (1896).
33. Prigg v. Pennsylvania, 16 Pet. 539 (1842).
34. Race Riots. (1975). In *Family encyclopedia of American history* (p. 919). Pleasantville, NY: Reader's Digest.

35. Railway Express Agency v. New York, 336 U.S. 106 (1949).
36. R.A.V. v. St. Paul, 505 U.S. 377 (1992).
37. Ridgeway, J. (1995). *Blood in the Face*. New York: Thunder's Mouth.
38. Rosenberg, D., and J. Kessler (2000). *Combatting extremism in cyberspace*. New York: Anti-Defamation League.
39. Rosenberg, D., and M. Lieberman (1999). *Hate Crime Laws: 2000*. New York: Anti-Defamation League.
40. Scott v. Sandford, 19 How. 393 (1857).
41. State v. Mann, 13 NC (2 Dev) 263 (1829).
42. State v. T.B.D., 656 So.2d 479 (Fla. 1995), *cert. denied,* 116 S. Ct. 1014 (1996).
43. Texas v. Johnson, 491 U.S. 397 (1989).
44. United States Commission on Civil Rights. (1983). *Intimidation and Violence— Racial and Religious Bigotry in America*. Washington, DC: Author.
45. United States v. Guest, 383 U.S. 745 (1966).
46. United States v. Price, 383 U.S. 787 (1966).
47. United States v. Reese, 92 U.S. 214 (1876).
48. Walker, S. (1994). *Hate Speech: The History of an American Controversy*. Lincoln, NE: Bison Books.
49. Watts v. United States, 394 U.S. 705 (1969).
50. Will, G. (1998, October 15). No Need to Broaden Federal Hate Crime Law. *Asbury Park Press,* p. A13.
51. Wisconsin v. Mitchell, 508 U.S. 476 (1993).

Corporate Crime Must Be Punished

George W. Bush

A surge of high profile criminal cases beginning in the 1990s increasingly brought the subject of "corporate crime" to public attention. Corporate crime covers a wide range of financial misdealings such as embezzlement, insider trading, securities fraud, and tax evasion, but it also includes acts such as wanton environmental destruction, the marketing of unapproved drugs and food, and gross neglect of employee health and safety. As the scope of corporate crime became increasingly evident, many began to argue that these criminal acts inflict more damage on society than all street crime combined. Certainly the numbers favor such an analysis: the Federal Bureau of Investigation estimated that in 2002 the cost of robbery, burglary, larceny-theft, motor vehicle theft, and arson was less than $18 billion while various studies have suggested that the costs of corporate crime in the same year were upwards of $400 billion.

In the following speech delivered by George W. Bush in 2002, the U.S. president argues that this tidal wave of corporate crime hurts not only the employees, retirees, and investors who suffer economic losses from such fraudulent behavior, but it also damages the confidence that underpins the capitalist economic system. In order to restore confidence in the character and conduct of business leaders, Bush announces the creation of a Corporate Fraud Task Force, tougher penalties for corporate fraud, and greater transparency of public accounting.

The American economy—our economy—is built on confidence. The conviction that our free enterprise system will continue to be the most powerful and most promising in the

George W. Bush, "President Announces Tough New Enforcement Initiatives for Reform: Remarks by the President on Corporate Responsibility," Office of the Press Secretary, July 9, 2002. www.whitehouse.gov.

world. That confidence is well-placed. After all, American technology is the most advanced in the world. Our universities attract the talent of the world. Our workers and ranchers and farmers can compete with anyone in the world. Our society rewards hard work and honest ambition, bringing people to our shores from all around the world who share those values. The American economy is the most creative and enterprising and productive system ever devised. . . .

We have much to be confident about in America. Yet our economy and our country need one more kind of confidence—confidence in the character and conduct of all of our business leaders. The American economy today is rising, while faith in the fundamental integrity of American business leaders is being undermined. Nearly every week brings better economic news, and a discovery of fraud and scandal—problems long in the making, but now coming to light.

We've learned of some business leaders obstructing justice, and misleading clients, falsifying records, business executives breaching the trust and abusing power. We've learned of CEOs earning tens of millions of dollars in bonuses just before their companies go bankrupt, leaving employees and retirees and investors to suffer. The business pages of American newspapers should not read like a scandal sheet.

The vast majority of businessmen and women are honest. They do right by their employees and their shareholders. They do not cut ethical corners, and their work helps create an economy which is the envy of the world.

Capitalism Must Be Principled

Yet high-profile acts of deception have shaken people's trust. Too many corporations seem disconnected from the values of our country. These scandals have hurt the reputations of many good and honest companies. They have hurt the stock market. And worst of all, they are hurting millions of people who depend on the integrity of businesses for their livelihood and their retirement, for their peace of mind and their financial well-being.

When abuses like this begin to surface in the corporate world, it is time to reaffirm the basic principles and rules that make capitalism work: truthful books and honest people, and well-enforced laws against fraud and corruption. All investment is an act of faith, and faith is earned by integrity. In the long run, there's no capitalism without conscience; there is no wealth without character.

And so again today I'm calling for a new ethic of personal responsibility in the business community; an ethic that will increase investor confidence, will make employees proud of their companies, and again, regain the trust of the American people.

Our nation's most respected business leaders. . . take this ethic very seriously. The Business Roundtable, the New York Stock Exchange, the NASDAQ have all proposed guidelines to improve corporate conduct and transparency. These include requirements that independent directors compose a majority of a company's board; that all members of audit, nominating, and compensation committees be independent; and that all stock option plans be approved by the shareholders. I call on all the stock markets to adopt these sensible reforms—these common-sense reforms—as soon as possible.

Identifying Fraud

Self-regulation is important, but it's not enough. Government cannot remove risk from investment—I know that—or chance from the market. But government can do more to promote transparency and ensure that risks are honest. And government can ensure that those who breach the trust of the American people are punished.

Bold, well-considered reforms should demand integrity, without stifling innovation and economic growth. From the antitrust laws of the nineteenth century to the S&L reforms of recent times, America has tackled financial problems when they appeared. The actions I'm proposing follow in this tradition, and should be welcomed by every honest company in America.

First, we will use the full weight of the law to expose and root out corruption. My administration will do everything in our power to end the days of cooking the books, shading the truth, and breaking our laws.

Today, by executive order, I create a new Corporate Fraud Task Force, headed by the Deputy Attorney General, which will target major accounting fraud and other criminal activity in corporate finance. The task force will function as a financial crimes SWAT team, overseeing the investigation of corporate abusers and bringing them to account.

I'm also proposing tough new criminal penalties for corporate fraud. This legislation would double the maximum prison terms for those convicted of financial fraud from five to ten years. Defrauding investors is a serious offense, and the punishment must be as serious as the crime. I ask Congress to strengthen the ability of SEC [Securities and Exchange Commission] investigators to temporarily freeze improper payments to corporate executives, and to strengthen laws that prevent the destruction of corporate documents in order to hide crimes.

Second, we're moving corporate accounting out of the shadows, so the investing public will have a true and fair and timely picture of assets and liabilities and income of publicly traded companies. Greater transparency will expose bad companies and, just as importantly, protect the reputations of the good ones. . . .

Punishing Deceit

Corporate officers who benefit from false accounting statements should forfeit all money gained by their fraud. An executive whose compensation is tied to his company's performance makes more money when his company does well—

that's fine, and that's fair when the accounting is above-board. Yet when a company uses deception—deception accounting to hide reality, executives should lose all their compensation—all their compensation—gained by the deceit.

Corporate leaders who violate the public trust should never be given that trust again. The SEC should be able to punish corporate leaders who are convicted of abusing their powers by banning them from ever serving again as officers or directors of a publicly held corporation. If an executive is guilty of outright fraud, resignation is not enough. Only a ban on serving at the top of another company will protect other shareholders and employees.

My accountability plan also requires CEOs to personally vouch for their firms' annual financial statements. Currently, a CEO signs a nominal certificate, and does so merely on behalf of the company. In the future, the signature of the CEO should also be his or her personal certification of the veracity and fairness of the financial disclosures. When you sign a statement, you're pledging your word, and you should stand behind it.

And because the shareholders of America need confidence in financial disclosures right away, the SEC has ordered the leaders of nearly a thousand large public companies to certify that the financial information they submitted in the last year was fair and it was accurate.

I've also called on the SEC to adopt new rules to ensure that auditors will be independent and not compromised by conflicts of interest.

The House of Representatives has passed needed legislation to encourage transparency and accountability in American businesses. The Senate also needs to act quickly and responsibly, so I can sign a good bill into law.

Enforcing Honesty

Third, my administration will guard the interests of small investor and pension holders. More than 80 million Americans own stock, and many of them are new to the market. Buying stock gives them an opportunity to build wealth over the long-term, and this is the very kind of responsible investment we must promote in America. To encourage stock ownership, we must make sure that analysts give honest advice, and pension plans treat workers fairly.

Stock analysts should be trusted advisors, not salesmen with a hidden agenda. We must prevent analysts from touting weak companies because they happen to be clients of their own firm for underwriting or merger advice. This is a flat-out conflict of interest, and we'll aggressively enforce new SEC rules against this practice. . . .

And the stock markets should make sure that the advice analysts give, and the terms they use, have real meaning to investors. "Buy" should not be the only word in an analyst's vocabulary. And they should never say "hold" when they really mean "sell." . . .

The Need for Principled Leadership

Tougher laws and stricter requirements will help—it will help. Yet, ultimately, the ethics of American business depend on the conscience of America's business leaders. We need men and women of character, who know the difference between ambition and destructive greed, between justified risk and irresponsibility, between enterprise and fraud.

Our schools of business must be principled teachers of right and wrong, and not surrender to moral confusion and relativism. Our leaders of business must set high and clear expectations of conduct, demonstrated by their own conduct. Responsible business leaders do not jump ship during hard times. Responsible leaders do not collect huge bonus packages when the value of their company dramatically declines. Responsible leaders do not take home tens of millions of dollars in compensation as their companies prepare to file for bankruptcy, devastating the holdings of their investors.

Everyone in a company should live up to high standards. But the burden of leadership rightly belongs to the chief executive officer. CEOs set the ethical direction for their companies. They set a moral tone by the decisions they make, the respect they show their employees, and their willingness to be held accountable for their actions. They set a moral tone by showing their disapproval of other executives who bring discredit to the business world. . . .

Self Regulation

Those who sit on corporate boards have responsibilities. I urge board members to check the quality of their company's financial statements; to ask tough questions about accounting methods; to demand that audit firms are not beholden to the CEO; and to make sure the compensation for senior executives squares with reality and common sense. And I challenge compensation committees to put an end to all company loans to corporate officers.

Shareholders also need to make their voices heard. They should demand an attentive and active board of directors. They should demand truly independent directors. They should demand that compensation committees reward long-term success, not failure. Shareholders should demand accountability not just in bad times, but especially in boom times, when accountability frequently breaks down. Shareholders are a company's most important constituency, and they should act like it.

The 1990s was a decade of tremendous economic growth. As we're now learning, it was also a decade when the promise of rapid profits allowed the seeds of scandal to spring up. A lot of money was made, but too often standards were tossed aside. Yet the American system of enterprise has not failed us. Some dishonest individuals have failed our system. Now comes the urgent work of enforcement and reform, driven by a new ethic of responsibility.

We will show that markets can be both dynamic and honest, that lasting wealth and prosperity are built on a foundation of integrity. By reasserting the best values of our country, we will reclaim the promise of our economy.

Criminal Law Has Been Overextended

Erik Luna

The state of Indiana bans the dyeing of birds and rabbits. Delaware punishes the sale of perfume or lotion as a beverage with a sentence of up to six months imprisonment. Anonymously sending an indecent or "suggestive" message in South Carolina will result in a sentence of up to three years imprisonment. Every year new activities are criminalized with the result that over the past century the number of crimes in most state penal codes has at least doubled in a phenomenon analysts have labelled "overcriminalization." This term does not only cover the addition of new crimes to the penal code but the increased use of the legal system to prosecute activities that could be dealt with without recourse to law enforcement. Recent examples include the arrest of a 61-year-old California grandmother for allowing street-side bushes to grow more than two feet high, the arrest of a woman in Washington D.C. for talking loudly on her cell phone, and the arrest of two Florida third-graders for drawing threatening pictures of a classmate.

In the following 2003 essay Erik Luna, a professor of law at the University of Utah, argues that overcriminalization is the result of politics, because politicians who propose tougher laws and stiffer sentences win favor with the public. Luna attests that the net effect of this continuing revision of the penal code has resulted in a labyrinth of laws that has little to do with punishing criminal behavior, but rather is an attempt to regulate society. And while some would argue that a complex law code ensures that the variety of criminal behaviors are dealt with adequately, Luna counters that over-criminalization weakens the moral force

Erik Luna, "Overextending the Criminal Law," *Cato Policy Report*, vol. xxv, no. 6, November–December 2003, pp. 1–16. www.cato.org. Copyright © 2003 Cato Institute. All rights reserved. Reproduced by permission.

of the criminal law to deal with serious crime because it no longer represents a well-understood and indisputable statement of shared norms.

Nothing is certain, Ben Franklin once said, but death and taxes. Had he lived during our time, Franklin might have added a few other certainties—and almost assuredly among them would have been the concept of "crime." By this, I am not referring to the rate of violence and unlawful deprivations of property or privacy in the United States, which ebbs and flows from year to year and decade to decade, often coinciding with dips in the economy or spikes in the number of young males in the general population. Instead, it is the troubling phenomenon of continually adding new crimes or more severe punishments to the penal code, criminalizing, recriminalizing, and overcriminalizing all forms of conduct, much of it innocuous, to the point of erasing the line between tolerable and unacceptable behavior.

The Laugh Test

Where once the criminal law might have stood as a well-understood and indisputable statement of shared norms in American society, now there is only a bloated compendium that looks very much like the dreaded federal tax code. The end results can be downright ugly: a soccer mom thrown in jail in a small Texas town for failing to wear a seatbelt; a 12-year-old girl arrested and handcuffed for eating french fries in a Metro station in Washington, D.C.; and defendants serving 2.5-year to life sentences in California prisons for, among other things, pilfering a slice of pizza.

These incidents may seem like outliers, the exceptions rather than the rule. And to be sure, every U.S. jurisdiction has on its books a set of crimes and punishment that are incontrovertible, involving acts and attendant mental states that must be prescribed in order to constitute a just society—

murdcr, rape, robbery, arson, and the like. But beyond those so-called common law crimes is a seemingly endless list of behaviors that, at a minimum, do not seem well suited for the penal code and at times appear to fall within a zone of personal liberty that should be outside the state's coercive powers. Moreover, the sheer number of idiosyncratic laws and the scope of discretionary enforcement might give reason to wonder whether the exceptions have become the rule.

Some crimes barely pass the laugh test. New Mexico makes it a misdemeanor to claim that a product contains honey unless it is made of "pure honey produced by honeybees." Florida criminalizes the display of deformed animals and the peddling of untested sparklers, as well as the mutilation of the Confederate flag for "crass or commercial purposes." Pretending to be a member of the clergy is a misdemeanor in Alabama, and Kentucky bans the use of reptiles during religious services. Maine prohibits the catching of crustaceans with anything but "conventional lobster traps," Colorado makes it a misdemeanor to hunt wildlife from an aircraft, and Texas declares it a felony to trip a horse or "seriously overwork" an animal. In turn, California forbids "three card monte" and, as a general rule, cheating at card games, while it's a crime in Illinois to camp on the side of a public highway or offer a movie for rent without clearly displaying its rating. Add to those gems countless local offenses, such as playing Frisbee on Galveston beaches after being warned by a lifeguard, molesting monarch butterflies in Pacific Grove, California, failing to return library books in Salt Lake City, or annoying birds in the parks of Honolulu.

Less comical but certainly more pervasive and consequential are the so-called vice crimes that have exasperated generations of American liberations. These offenses are marked by the absence of violence or coercion, with parties engaged in voluntary transactions for desired goods or services. This category would include the possession, sale, or use of illegal drugs; acts of prostitution and other commercialized sexual conduct; transactions involving pornography or allegedly obscene materials; and all kinds of gambling activities. Government has also banned behaviors that are related to vice or seen as precursors, for example, the possession of drug paraphernalia such as pipes and spoons and loitering in public places with the apparent intent to sell drugs or turn tricks. Congress has even considered a bill that would make it a federal crime to throw a party where drugs might be used.

Criminalizing Business

Other growth areas for the penal code include regulatory or business-related offenses and crimes involving misrepresentation and the like. Today's administrative state has created a massive web of laws concerning trade, labor, product and workplace safety, environmental protection, securities regulation, housing, transportation, and so on, often backed by the criminal sanction. Many of the statutes may make a good deal of sense—for example, prohibiting modern iterations on the common law crime of larceny. Others seem a bit silly, such as the infamous federal crimes of removing mattress tags and the unauthorized use of "Smokey Bear" or "Woodsy Owl." But many regulatory offenses—filing an inaccurate monitoring report under the Clean Water Act or being in a position of responsibility when an employee violates regulations of the FDA, EPA, SEC, and other acronym agencies—place otherwise honest folks in real jeopardy. As Berkeley law professor Sanford Kadish once noted, some economic crime, such as violations of securities regulations, antitrust statutes, and unfair competition laws, more "closely resembles acceptable aggressive business behavior." In turn, mail and wire fraud statutes have been expanded to seemingly irrational ends, covering conduct that amounts to little more than breaches of fiduciary duty. In one case, a college professor was convicted of mail fraud for awarding degrees to students who plagiarized others' work.

Beyond the truly novel are offenses that merely recriminalize or overcriminalize conduct that is already prohibited. Many penal codes contain dozens of provisions covering the same basic crime—assault, theft, sex offenses, arson, and so on—each provision dealing with an allegedly unique scenario but in fact just retreading the same conduct. Politically inspired offenses fall within this category as well, with, for instance, "carjacking" more than well covered by proscriptions on robbery and kidnapping. Penal code machinations have also involved drastic expansions in punishment, most notably the enactment of mandatory minimum sentences for narcotics crimes and anti-recidivist statutes along the lines of "three strikes and you're out." And after factoring in various liability-expanding doctrines, such as conspiracy and solicitation, the reach and force of the criminal law and its penalties can be awe inspiring and disconcerting. . . .

Why the Urge to Criminalize?

Any number of explanations can be offered for America's drive to criminalize, its appetite for a crime-of-the-month. Part of the rationale likely stems from a slow but certain movement away from common law principles of crime and punishment and toward a larger ambit for the criminal justice system. To simplify a bit, the common law required a convergence of harmful conduct (*actus reus*) and a culpable mental state (*mens rea*). As an example, larceny involved more than just taking someone's private property—the accused must have known that the object in question belonged to another and intended to deprive him of that property. There were also fairly robust limitations on vicarious liability, whether a homeowner could be criminally culpable for the actions of his drunken visitor, for instance, or the businessman could be liable for the wrongful deeds of his employee. Today, however, criminal responsibility can be doled out without a culpable mental state through the concept of "strict liability," and corporate managers can be held liable for serious offenses without evidence of personal guilt. An honest and reasonable claim of "I didn't know" is often deemed irrelevant, despite the mind-boggling number of administrative regulations that carry criminal sanctions. . . .

Probably the most powerful explanation for the criminalization phenomenon is the one-way ratchet of law-and-order politics. To put it simply, lawmakers have every reason to add new crimes and punishments, which make great campaign fodder, but no countervailing political interest in cutting the penal code. The benefits of overcriminalization are concentrated on the political class, providing nice sound bites and résumé filler at reelection time, while the costs are either diffuse (but very real, as will be discussed below) or borne by discrete and insular minorities without a way in the political process, such as members of lower socioeconomic classes or those accused of crime. Experience has shown that being tough on crime wins elections, and a sure-fire way to look tough is to add a superfluous carjacking statute or boost the penalty for drug dealers, irrespective of the statute's normative justification or ultimate effect on society. And once on the books, criminal laws are virtually impossible to rescind (consider, for instance, the continued existence of anti-dueling statutes). . . .

The Costs of Overcriminalization

The costs and consequences of over-criminalization are many and, in many cases, all too obvious—but let me briefly mention a few. To begin with, a bloated penal code and overly broad criminal liability are unhealthy for an adversarial system of criminal justice, where law enforcers are not neutral and detached but instead interested parties actively seeking arrests and convictions. Overcriminalization leads to enormous police discretion to stop pedestrians or motorists using legal pretexts, which serve as cover for discriminatory enforcement based on class, race, or ethnicity. As observed by racial profiling scholar David Harris, no driver could cover more than three blocks without violating some traffic law, thereby providing a pretense for an elongated detention and extensive search. For prosecutors, overcriminalization results in a total imbalance of arms, with severe punishment, often in the form of mandatory minimums or habitual offender statutes, used as leverage in extracting information or guilty pleas. Prosecutorial domination via overcriminalization is bad enough when the underlying offense and attached penalties are dubious to begin with (drug crimes being the paradigmatic case for libertarians like myself). But the sledgehammer of draconian punishment is most disturbing when it is used to coax pleas out of individuals with valid claims of mitigation or even innocence, an unsettling situation that has proven to be all too common.

Overcriminalization also has the potential to squander or misallocate scarce resources, particularly when the underlying offense—a vice crime, for example—causes little direct harm. "One can imagine side effects of the effort to enforce morality by penal law," Professor Louis Schwartz of the University of Pennsylvania wondered some forty years ago, "Are police forces, prosecution resources, and court time being wastefully diverted from the central insecurities of our metropolitan life—robbery, burglary, rape, assault, and governmental corruption?" The answer is the same today as it was then: Resources spent chasing the otherwise innocuous prostitute and panderer, for instance, could be spent instead in pursuit of the real sex criminals—the rapist and the child molester. And, of course, the billions of dollars wasted on the so-called war on drugs would be better spent on a different, much graver battle: the "war on terror" and the pursuit of those who would fly commercial airliners into American skyscrapers, set off bombs in public venues and government buildings, and release biochemical weapons through mail, commerce, or public works.

Weakening Respect for Law

Most of all, overcriminalization weakens the moral force of the criminal law. By "moral," I am not referring to big-M Morality, as in the occasionally obnoxious religiosity of the "Moral Majority," but instead the shared norms of American society as to what should or should not be subject to the single most powerful action any government can take: the deprivation of human liberty or even life itself. That is, after all, what a penal code should be about—a communal decision that certain behaviors, pursuant to certain mental states, are so violent or harmful to their direct victims and society at large as to justify the social reprobation and deprivation of liberty that accompany the adjudication of guilt. When the criminal sanction is used for conduct that is widely viewed as harmless or undeserving of the severest condemnation, the moral force of the penal code is diminished, possibly to the point of near irrelevance among some individuals and groups. It fails to distinguish between the acceptable and the intolerable, between the lawful and the illicit. And it no longer deters *ex ante*, before crime, but only catalogs punishment *ex post*, at trial and at sentencing when the damage has already been done. Unwarranted bans or penalties can fulfill none of the valid goals of the criminal sanction, namely, preventing future harmful conduct and justly punishing individuals for past wrongdoing.

Before another offense or punishment is added to the penal code, we should start asking ourselves, Is this really necessary or just another crime-of-the-month?

Capital Punishment Is Just and Effective

Cass R. Sunstein and Adrian Vermeule

Of primary concern in the ongoing debate about capital punishment is the issue of whether capital punishment deters crime. In the following selection, law professors Cass Sunstein and Adrian Vermeule utilize current econometric research to argue that capital punishment does have a deterrent effect on crime. Furthermore, they find that this deterrent effect has a praise mathematical consequence which means that each execution of a criminal results in up to 18 fewer murders. From this evidence the authors draw the surprising conclusion that by banning capital punishment a government sentences untold numbers of innocent victims to death by murder at the hands of violent criminals who would otherwise been deterred. Sunstein and Vermeule argue that because these additional deaths happen arbitrarily and without fair process, their victims deserve more consideration than the deaths of convicts who have passed through a fair legal process. Because of this Sunstein and Vermeule argue that capital punishment is not only morally permissible, but morally required.

Many people believe capital punishment is morally impermissible. In their view, executions are inherently cruel and barbaric. Often they add that capital punishment is not, and cannot be, imposed in a way that adheres to the rule of law. They contend that as administered, capital punishment ensures the execution of (some) innocent people, and also that it reflects arbitrariness, in the form of random or invidious infliction of the ultimate penalty.

Cass R. Sunstein and Adrian Vermeule, "Is Capital Punishment Morally Required? The Relevance of Life-Life Tradeoffs," *Stanford Law Review*, January 2006. Republished with permission of *Stanford Law Review*, conveyed through Copyright Clearance Center, Inc. and the authors.

Defenders of capital punishment come in two different camps. Some are retributivists. Following [German philosopher Immanuel] Kant, they claim that for the most heinous forms of wrongdoing, the penalty of death is morally justified or perhaps even required. Other defenders of capital punishment are consequentialists and often also welfarists. They contend that the deterrent effect of capital punishment is significant and that it justifies the infliction of the ultimate penalty. Consequentialist defenses of capital punishment, however, tend to assume that capital punishment is (merely) morally permissible, as opposed to being morally obligatory.

Our goal here is to suggest that the debate over capital punishment is rooted in an unquestioned assumption, and that the failure to question that assumption is a serious moral error. The assumption is that for governments, acts are morally different from omissions. We want to raise the possibility that an indefensible form of the act-omission distinction is crucial to the most prominent objections to capital punishment—and that defenders of capital punishment, apparently making the same distinction, have failed to notice that on the logic of their theory, capital punishment is morally obligatory, not just permissible. We want to suggest, in other words, that capital punishment may be morally required not for retributive reasons, but in order to prevent the taking of innocent lives.

The suggestion bears not only on moral and political debates, but also on constitutional questions. In invalidating the death penalty for juveniles, for example, the Supreme Court did not seriously engage the possibility that capital punishment for juveniles may help to prevent the death of innocents, including the deaths of juvenile innocents. And if our suggestion is correct, it is connected to many questions outside of the context of capital punishment. If omissions by the state are often indistinguishable, in principle, from actions by the state, then a wide range of apparent failures to act—in the context not only of criminal and civil law, but of regulatory law as well—should be taken to raise serious moral and legal problems. Those who accept our arguments in favor of the death penalty may or may not welcome the implications for government action in general. In many situations, ranging from environmental quality to highway safety to relief of poverty, our arguments suggest that in light of imaginable empirical findings, government is obliged to provide far more protection than it now does, and that it should not be permitted to hide behind unhelpful distinctions between acts and omissions.

The foundation for our argument is a large and growing body of evidence that capital punishment may well have a deterrent effect, possibly a quite powerful one. A leading study suggests that each execution prevents some eighteen murders, on average. The particular numbers do not much matter. If the current evidence is even roughly correct, then a refusal to impose capital punishment will effectively condemn numerous innocent people to death. States that choose life imprisonment, when they might choose capital punishment, are ensuring the deaths of a large number of innocent people. On moral grounds, a choice that effectively condemns large numbers of people to death seems objectionable to say the least. For those who are inclined to be skeptical of capital punishment for moral reasons—a group that includes one of the current authors—the task is to consider the possibility that the failure to impose capital punishment is, prima facie and all things considered, a serious moral wrong. . . .

The Evidence

For many years, the deterrent effect of capital punishment was sharply disputed. But a great deal of recent evidence strengthens the claim that capital punishment has large deterrent effects. The reason for the shift is that a wave of sophisticated econometric studies have exploited a newly available form of data, so-called "panel data" that uses all information from a set of units (states or counties) and follows that data over an extended period of time. A leading study used county-level panel data from 3,054 U.S. counties between 1977 and 1996. The authors find that the murder rate is significantly reduced by both death sentences and executions. The most striking finding is that *on average, each execution results in eighteen fewer murders.*

Other econometric studies also find a substantial deterrent effect. In two papers, [economist] Paul Zimmerman uses state-level panel data from 1978 onwards to measure the deterrent effect of execution rates and execution methods. He estimates that each execution deters an average of fourteen murders. Using state-level data from 1977 to 1997, [economists Naci] Mocan and [Kaj] Gittings find that each execution deters five murders on average. They also find that increases in the murder rate come from removing people from death row and also from commutations in death sentences. Yet another study, based on state-level data from 1997–1999, finds that a death sentence deters 4.5 murders and an execution deters 3 murders. The same study investigates the question whether executions deter crimes of passion and murders by intimates. The answer is clear: these categories of murder are deterred by capital punishment. The deterrent effect of the death penalty is also found to be a function of the length of waits on death row, with a murder deterred for every 2.75 years of reduction in the period before execution.

In the period between 1972 and 1976, the Supreme Court produced an effective moratorium on capital punishment, and an extensive study exploits that fact to estimate the deterrent effect. Using state-level data from 1960–2000, the authors make before-and-after comparisons, focusing on the murder rate in each state before and after the death penalty was suspended and reinstated. The authors find a substantial deterrent effect. After suspending the death penalty, 91 percent of states faced an increase in homicides—and in 67 percent of states, the rate was decreased after reinstatement of capital punishment. . . .

The Death Penalty and Race

Some people believe that even if capital punishment could be morally acceptable if it were fairly administered, the inevitability of unfair administration means that we must eliminate it. These arguments point to strong reasons for reforming the existing system to increase accuracy and decrease arbitrariness. But the arguments do not succeed as objections to capital punishment as such. Once the act-omission distinction is no longer central, it becomes clear that *the standard moral objections to capital punishment apply even more powerfully to the murders that capital punishment prevents.* Those murders also cause irreversible deaths: the deaths of the victims of murder. Private murders are also often highly arbitrary, involving selectivity on any number of morally irrelevant or objectionable grounds. African-Americans, for example, are far more likely than other groups to be the victims of murder. In 2003, 48 percent of murder victims were white and 48 percent were African-American—meaning that the racial disparity in the probability of becoming a murder victim is even greater than the racial disparity in the probability of ending up on death row. An important corollary is that the benefits of capital punishment, to the extent that it operates as a powerful deterrent of murder, are likely to flow disproportionately to African-Americans.

To be sure, this effect will be attenuated if death sentences are imposed less frequently on those who murder African-Americans. In the most pessimistic projection, capital punishment is likely to be disproportionately inflicted on African-Americans, and because that punishment is most likely to be imposed when whites have been killed, the resulting savings are likely to go largely to whites. On this view, the "life-life tradeoffs" may turn out, all too often, to be "African-American life–white-life tradeoffs." Perhaps it is unclear how to make that tradeoff, even if it involves larger numbers, and innocence, on one side of the ledger. But even on the current numbers, this projection is unrealistic. Most murder is intraracial, not interracial. Because African-Americans are disproportionately the victims of homicide, and because their murderers are disproportionately African-American, they have a great deal to gain from capital punishment—very plausibly more, on balance, than white people do. In any event, the more natural response to existing racial disparities is to lower them, rather than to eliminate the penalty altogether.

A Life-Life Tradeoff

For the rule of law questions, as for all others, the core problem of capital punishment is that it presents a risk-risk tradeoff, or a life-life tradeoff. To say the least, it is extremely desirable to prevent arbitrary or irreversible deaths, but this consideration is on both sides of the ledger. The relevant analogy is not, say, to a policy that uses racial classifications to increase security or national wealth. The closer analogy would be one that uses racial classifications in order to minimize the overall use of racial classifications, or to hasten the day when racial classifications are no longer useful. A still closer analogy would be a policy that increases certain risks but that in the process decreases other risks of greater magnitude. Whatever the merits of such tradeoffs across different settings, a one-sided complaint about a harm or loss that is on both sides of the ledger is not a sufficient objection to a policy of this sort.

On this view, the crucial point is that a legal regime with capital punishment predictably produces far *fewer* arbitrary and irreversible deaths than a regime without capital punishment. In a sensible regime of capital punishment, legal rules, enforced by administrative, judicial and citizen oversight, attempt to reduce arbitrariness and error up to the point where further reductions would inflict unacceptable harms. Where killing is carried out by private parties, however, there are no such institutions for keeping arbitrariness in check. Most striking is the sheer size of the opportunity cost of foregone capital punishment. Stipulate that for every foregone execution (conducted under procedural safeguards), the cost is on average, some eighteen arbitrary and irreversible murders. . . . Suppose, for example, that five hundred additional death row inmates were executed in the next year. Unless the marginal deterrent benefit of each additional execution diminishes very rapidly, the result would be to save thousands of innocent people—in all probability, far more people than were killed in the terrorist attacks of September 11, 2001. The people whose lives are lost, and whose deaths could be averted, are killed arbitrarily and without fair process. In short, rule-of-law criticisms of capital punishment either smuggle in the distinction between acts and omissions, or else overlook the fact that the same objections apply even more powerfully to the utterly arbitrary killings that capital punishment prevents.

Chronology

1791

The Second Amendment, which grants the "right of the people to keep and bear arms," is ratified.

1821

Connecticut passes the first law in the United States banning abortions after "quickening," that is, before the fetus has moved in the womb, generally in the fourth or fifth month. By the end of the century, most states had banned abortions outright.

1829

First experiment in solitary confinement in the United States begins at the Eastern State Penitentiary in Philadelphia.

1868

The United Kingdom enacts the world's first anti-drug law, which prohibits the selling of opium without a license.

1909

Opium is criminalized in the U.S.

1920

The production, sale, and transportation of alcoholic beverages are outlawed, beginning a period of U.S. history known as prohibition.

1933

The U.S. federal ban on alcohol is removed.

1936

Last public execution occurs before a crowd of 20,000 in Owensboro, Kentucky.

1939

Edwin Sutherland coins the term "white-collar crime."

1966

Public support for the death penalty reaches an all-time low, with only 42% of the population in favor of continuing the practice.

1971

President Richard Nixon declares a "war on drugs."

1972

The Supreme Court rules that allowing a jury the discretion to decide between death or life imprisonment upon conviction of murder is unconstitutional. The practical effect of the ruling is the overturning of all existing death-penalty laws and sentences.

1973

New York State introduces mandatory minimum sentences for the possession of hard drugs. The minimum sentence of 15 years to life is widely criticized as unjustly punitive.

In *Roe v. Wade*, the Supreme Court strikes down a Texas law banning abortion, decriminalizing the practice in the first 13 weeks of pregnancy.

1976

The Supreme Court reinstates the death penalty in ruling that where the jury's discretion is carefully guided to consider aggravating and mitigating circumstances, the death penalty does not violate the Constitution.

1977

The Supreme Court rules that the use of the death penalty in rape cases reflects disproportionate punishment.

1986

The Supreme Court bans the executing of insane persons.

1990

The Federal Bureau of Investigation begins to collect statistics on hate crimes.

1992

The U.S. crime rate begins to decline.

1993

Washington becomes the first state to enact a "three strikes" law. The law requires the court to hand down mandatory life sentences for three-time violent offenders.

President Bill Clinton signs the Brady Bill, which institutes mandatory background checks for handgun purchases.

The Supreme Court rules that hate crime laws are constitutional, arguing that "bias-motivated offenses warrant greater maximum penalties across the board."

1994

Californian voters approve Proposition 184, a controversial "three strikes" law. Unlike Washington's version, the three crimes need not be violent, but simply a felony. Furthermore, the law doubles minimum terms for second-time offenders.

Public support for the death penalty reaches an all-time high, with 80% of the population in favor of continuing the practice.

New York City Mayor Rudolph Giuliani and Police Commissioner William Bratton institute a "zero tolerance" policing initiative motivated by the idea that aggressive law enforcement of petty disorder will result in a reduction of serious crime.

1999

Fourteen students and one teacher are killed at Columbine High School in Littleton, Colorado, provoking debate regarding gun control, school security, and "zero tolerance" policies.

2001

President George W. Bush signs the USA PATRIOT Act into law. Created in response to the September 11, 2001, terror attacks, the Act dramatically expands the authority of law enforcement.

Energy corporation Enron declares bankruptcy after widespread false-accounting practices come to light. The implications of the scandal have far-reaching effects on the business community, and Enron becomes a symbol of corporate corruption.

2002

The U.S. prison population tops two million, hitting an all-time high.

The Supreme Court prohibits the execution of the severely retarded.

Telecom giant WorldCom's multi-billion dollar accounting fraud is revealed.

In response to corporate corruption scandals exemplified by Enron and WorldCom, President George W. Bush establishes the Corporate Fraud Task Force to expose and punish corruption.

2004

Following a decade of decline, violent crime reaches the lowest level ever recorded.

2005

The Supreme Court abolishes the death penalty for crimes committed by convicts who were under 18 at the time of the crime.

2006

Congress renews the USA PATRIOT Act.

South Dakota bans all abortions except those done to save the life of the mother, in an explicit challenge to the Supreme Court's 1973 decision.

Organizations to Contact

Coalition to Stop Gun Violence (CSGV)
1023 15th St. NW, Suite 301, Washington, DC   20005
(202) 408-0061
Web site: www.csgv.org

The CSGV is committed to the reduction of gun violence through the advocacy of legislation that regulates firearm distribution. The CSGV Web site provides a comprehensive list of reports, publications, and statistics related to gun violence.

Death Penalty Information Center (DPIC)
1101 Vermont Ave. NW, Suite 701, Washington, DC   20005
(202) 289-2275 • fax: (202) 289-7336
Web site: www.deathpenaltyinfo.org

The DPIC provides analysis and information on issues concerning capital punishment from federal reports, independent studies, and scholarly articles. The DPIC's Web site includes information concerning capital crimes by state, the history of the death penalty, and a variety of statistics concerning those executed.

Families Against Mandatory Minimums (FAMM)
1612 K St. NW, Suite 700, Washington, DC   20006
(202) 822-6700 • fax: (202) 822-6704
e-mail: famm@famm.org
Web site: www.famm.org

FAMM promotes flexible sentencing policies that give judges the discretion to apply punishments that take into account the particularities of the defendant's role in the offense, the seriousness of the offense, and the potential for rehabilitation. FAMM's primary goal is the eradication of mandatory-minimum sentencing laws and the restoration of judicial discretion.

Federal Bureau of Investigation (FBI)
J. Edgar Hoover Building, 935 Pennsylvania Ave. NW
Washington, DC   20535-0001
(202) 324-3000
Web site: www.fbi.gov

The FBI is charged with the duty "to protect and defend the United States against terrorist and foreign intelligence threats and to enforce the criminal laws of the United States." To this end, its Intelligence Program is seen as the core of its investigative mission. An often-quoted and useful resource is the annual Uniform Crime Report, which provides statistics on crime offenses in cities and communities across the country.

National Center for Victims of Crime (NCVC)
2000 M St. NW, Suite 480, Washington, DC   20036
(202) 467-8700 • fax: (202) 467-8701
Web site: www.ncvc.org

The nation's leading resource and advocacy organization for crime victims, the NCVC collaborates with local, state, and federal partners to provide services and resources to victims. Additionally, the NCVC advocates for laws and public policies that secure rights and protections for the victims of crime.

National Crime Prevention Council (NCPC)
1000 Connecticut Ave. NW, 13th Flr., Washington, DC   20036
(202) 466-6272 • fax: (202) 296-1356
Web site: www.ncpc.org

The NCPC produces publications and teaching programs that address the causes of crime and violence in an effort to create safer communities. Though the mission of the organization is primarily educational, it also engages with a variety of federal and local agencies to combat the myriad root causes of crime.

National Criminal Justice Association (NCJA)
720 Seventh St. NW, 3rd Flr., Washington, DC   20001
(202) 628-8550 • fax: (202) 628-0080
Web site: www.ncja.org

The NCJA represents state, tribal, and local governments on crime-prevention and crime-control issues. It promotes a balanced approach to community public safety and criminal and juvenile justice system problems. The NCJA serves as the formal mechanism for informing Congress of state, tribal, and local criminal and juvenile justice needs and accomplishments.

National Rifle Association–Institute for Legislative Action (NRA–ILA)
11250 Waples Mill Rd., Fairfax, Virginia   22030
(800) 392-8683
Web site: www.nraila.org

The NRA–ILA is the lobbying arm of the National Rifle Association of America. It is committed to preserving the right of individuals to purchase, possess, and use firearms. The NRA–ILA's Web site contains a variety of reports and articles on the issues and laws concerning gun ownership.

Public Agenda
6 East 39th St., New York, New York   10016
(212) 686-6610 • fax: (212) 889-3461
Web site: www.publicagenda.org

Public Agenda is a nonpartisan opinion research organization dedicated to helping Americans understand a variety of critical issues. The "crime" section of the organization's Web site contains a wealth of information, from statistics to polls to discussions on all aspects of crime.

United Nations Office on Drugs and Crime (UNODC)
Vienna International Centre, PO Box 500, Vienna   A-1400
   Austria
+43 1 26060 0 • fax: +43 1 26060 5866
Web site: www.unodc.org

The UNODC is an international organization mandated to assist United Nations member states in their struggles against illicit drugs, crime, and terrorism. The UNODC produces research on drugs and crime issues, assists in the implementation of international treaties, and assists national governments in the fight against crime.

U.S. Department of Justice (DOJ)
950 Pennsylvania Ave. NW, Washington, DC   20530-0001
(202) 514-2000
e-mail: askdoj@usdoj.gov
Web site: www.usdoj.gov

The U.S. Department of Justice is mandated to enforce the laws of the United States and to ensure public safety against both foreign and domestic threats at the federal level. Represented by the office of the attorney general, the DOJ comprises many different agencies, including the Bureau of Alcohol, Tobacco, Firearms, and Explosives; the Drug Enforcement Administration; the Federal Bureau of Prisons; and the National Institute of Justice. The DOJ Web site holds many statistics and reports on crime in America.

For Further Research

Books

Robert Agnew, *Juvenile Delinquency; Causes and Control.* Los Angeles: Roxbury, 2000.

D.A. Andrews and James Bonta, *The Psychology of Criminal Conduct.* Cincinnati: Anderson, 1994.

Curt R. Bartol, *Criminal Behavior: A Psychosocial Approach.* Upper Saddle River, NJ: Prentice Hall, 1980.

Deborah R. Baskin and Ira B. Sommers, *Casualties of Community Disorder: Women's Careers in Violent Crime.* Boulder, CO: Westview, 1998.

William J. Bennett, John J. DiIulio Jr., and John P. Walters, *Body Count: Moral Poverty . . . and How to Win America's War Against Crime and Drugs.* New York: Simon & Schuster, 1996.

Alfred Blumstein and Joel Wallman, eds., *The Crime Drop in America.* New York: Cambridge University Press, 2000.

William J. Bratton with Peter Knobler, *Turnaround: How America's Top Cop Reversed the Crime Epidemic.* New York: Random House, 1998.

Elain Cassel and Douglas Bernstein, *Criminal Behavior.* Boston: Allyn & Bacon, 2001.

Ramsey Clark, *Crime in America: Observations on Its Nature, Causes, Prevention, and Control.* New York: Simon & Schuster, 1970.

Steven R. Donziger, ed., *The Real War on Crime: The Report of the National Criminal Justice Commission.* New York: HarperPerennial, 1996.

Amitai Etzioni, *How Patriotic Is the Patriot Act? Freedom Versus Security in the Age of Terrorism*. New York: Routledge, 2004.

Marcus Felson, *Crime and Nature*. Thousand Oaks, CA: Sage, 2006.

Nathan Hall, *Hate Crime*. Portland, OR: Willan, 2005.

Simon Hallsworth, *Street Crime*. Portland, OR: Willan, 2005.

Christopher Hibbert, *The Roots of Evil: A Social History of Crime and Punishment*. Westport, CT: Greenwood, 1978.

Ronald D. Hunter and Mark L. Dantzker, *Crime and Criminality: Causes and Consequences*. Upper Saddle River, NJ: Prentice Hall, 2002.

Yvonne Jewkes, ed., *Dot.cons: Crime, Deviance, and Identity on the Internet*. Portland, OR: Willan, 2003.

Peter Joyce, *Criminal Justice: An Introduction to Crime and the Criminal Justice System*. Portland, OR: Willan, 2006.

George L. Kelling and Catherine M. Coles, *Fixing Broken Windows*. New York: Simon & Schuster, 1998.

John Lott, *More Guns, Less Crime: Understanding Crime and Gun Control Laws*. Chicago: University of Chicago Press, 1998.

Jens Ludwig and Philip J. Cook, eds., *Evaluating Gun Policy: Effects on Crime and Violence*. Washington, DC: Brookings Institution, 2003.

Eugene McLaughlin and John Muncie, eds., *Controlling Crime*. Thousand Oaks, CA: Sage, 1996.

Kate Moss and Mike Stephens, eds., *Crime Reduction and the Law*. New York: Routledge, 2006.

Mike Nash, *Public Protection and the Criminal Justice Process*. New York: Oxford University Press, 2006.

Barbara Perry, *In the Name of Hate: Understanding Hate Crimes.* New York: Routledge, 2001.

Richard Quinney, *Class, State, and Crime.* New York: David McKay, 1977.

Sally S. Simpson, *Corporate Crime, Law, and Social Control.* New York: Cambridge University Press, 2002.

Basia Spalek, *Crime Victims: Theory, Policy and Practice.* New York: Palgrave Macmillan, 2006.

Periodicals

Richard M. Aborn, "Time to End Recidivism," *Nation*, March 4, 2005.

Dan P. Alsobrooks, "Waging a Battle Against the Myths," *Corrections Today*, December 2002.

William J. Bennett, "Don't Surrender," *Wall Street Journal*, May 15, 2001.

Brian Bergman, "Just Say 'Yes': Legalizing Marijuana Would Actually Be Safer for Kids than Decriminalization," *Maclean's*, March 3, 2003.

Mark Boal, "The Drug War's New Front," *Rolling Stone*, March 30, 2000.

Deanna Boyd and Melody McDonald, "Insanity on Trial," *Fort Worth Star-Telegram*, August 8, 2004.

George S. Bridges, "Different Strokes: Consciously or Not, the Legal System Doesn't Perceive Blacks and Whites the Same Way," *Seattle Post-Intelligencer*, March 7, 1999.

William F. Buckley Jr., "Look at the Money Saved if We Legalized Drugs!" *Buffalo News*, April 5, 1995.

Fox Butterfield, "New Drug-Offender Program Draws Unexpected Clients," *New York Times*, September 29, 2001.

Michael Duffy and Nancy Gibbs, "How Far Do We Want the FBI to Go?" *Time*, June 10, 2002.

Annabel Gillings, "Genes and Behaviour," *Prospect*, October, 1996.

Jim Gogek and Ed Gogek, "Freedom Behind Bars," *San Diego Union-Tribune*, June 4, 2000.

Brad A. Greenberg, "Patriot Act Carves Away Basic Rights," *San Bernardino Sun*, September 10, 2004.

Linda Greenhouse, "Supreme Court, 5-4, Forbids Execution in Juvenile Crime," *New York Times*, March 2, 2005.

Timothy Harper, "Shoot to Kill," *Atlantic Monthly*, October 2000.

David R. Henderson, "Supporting the Drug War Supports Terrorists," *Reason*, July 2002.

Morris B. Hoffman and Stephen J. Morse, "The Insanity Defense Goes Back on Trial," *New York Times*, July 30, 2006.

Matthew O. Howard, "Modern 'War on Drugs' Is Supported by Elemental Untruths," *Seattle Times*, May 2, 1990.

Brendan I. Koener, "Crime Out of Mind," *Village Voice*, August 29–September 4, 2001.

Joshua Kurlantzick, "Pirates of the Corporation," *Mother Jones*, July/August, 2005.

M.L. Lyke, "Number of Female Inmates Soars," *Seattle Post-Intelligencer*, March 5, 2003.

Heather MacDonald, "Crime, Not Race," *New York Post*, January 29, 2004.

Peter Shinkle, "Can the Feds Stop Gun Violence?" *St. Louis Post-Dispatch*, September 5, 2005.

James Sterngold and Mark Martin, "Hard Time," *San Francisco Chronicle*, July 3, 2005.

Margaret Talbot, "True Confessions," *Atlantic Monthly*, July/ August, 2002.

Winston Williams, "White-Collar Crime: Booming Again," *New York Times*, June 10, 1985.

Steven Wishnia, "What's Your Anti-Drug?" *In These Times*, April 16, 2001.

Kate Zernike, "Violent Crime Rising Sharply in Some Cities," *New York Times*, February 12, 2006.

Internet Sources

American Civil Liberties Union, "Race and the War on Drugs," September 17, 2003. www.aclu.org.

Peter Daniels, "US: Record Numbers in Prison and On Parole," August 3, 2004. www.wsws.org.

Yosef Edelstein, "A Few Reflections on Capital Punishment," June 23, 2000. www.ou.org.

Sean Gonsalves, "The Problem Is the Solution?" February 10, 2004. www.zmag.org.

Aghatise E. Joseph, "Cybercrime Definition," June 28, 2006. www.crime-research.org.

John Overington, "Capital Punishment: Its Time Has Come in WV," October 11, 2003. www.conservatives.org.

Steve Sailer, "Mapping the Unmentionable: Race and Crime," February 13, 2005. www.vdare.com.

Dudley Sharp, "Innocence Issues: The Death Penalty," April 16, 2000. www.prodeathpenalty.com.

U.S. Conference of Catholic Bishops, "Living the Gospel of Life: A Challenge to American Catholics," November 19, 1998. www.nccbuscc.org.

James Q. Wilson, "Legalizing Drugs Makes Matters Worse," September 1, 2000. www.slate.com.

Index